Argonauts of California

TOM ELLIOTT

BARBED WIRE PUBLISHING
LAS CRUCES, NEW MEXICO

Printed in the United States of America.

Published by Barbed Wire Publishing
1990 East Lohman Avenue, Suite 225
Las Cruces, New Mexico 88001 USA

Title font Caxton Book
Text font Bembo and ITC Legacy Sans
Book and cover design by Vicki Ligon

ISBN 0-9711930-4-5

1 2 3 4 5 6 7 8 9 0

Dedication

This book is dedicated to all people born in the Great State of California—past, present, and future—and to their parents, grandparents, and great-grandparents that had enough sense to move to California for the opportunities offered by this land of greatness. You are truly the Argonauts seeking The Golden Fleece—whether it be health, wealth, or climate.

In Greek mythology a band of heroes under the command of Admiral Jason, sailed on the Ship Argo seeking the golden and magical fleece from the winged ram. Their travels led them far and wide both by land and sea through the known world of the time, until these Argonauts accomplished their goal.

Bret Harte, the famous writer from the California gold field era of 1849 and a member of the realist school of writers, referred to the Argonauts in his writings as heroes that came from far afield, both by land and sea, seeking the treasure of the High Sierra. The golden fleece, of course, was not a sheepskin, but gold dust and nuggets that would make each individual wealthy.

BEST WISHES—
Tom Elliott

About the Author

Born and raised in West Los Angeles, Tom graduated from University High School. He attended the University of Oregon on a football and track scholarship, but because he was a Marine Corps reservist, his education was interrupted in 1950 at the outbreak of the Korean War.

On active duty in Korea, Tom participated in the amphibious assault of Inchon, South Korea, and later he survived the winter operation at the Chosin Reservoir in North Korea. After fourteen months of active duty he was discharged from the Marine Corps and returned to his studies at the University of Oregon where he graduated in 1954.

He joined the management training program of the Union Oil Company of California and was soon promoted to Supervisor of Retail Sales in Portland, Oregon. He transferred to the San Francisco division where he was responsible for retail operations north of the Bay Area.

Tom was presented with an opportunity to change careers so he left the petroleum industry and joined the Transamerica Life Companies in San Francisco. Over the next forty years of his career Tom held positions as Assistant Branch Manager in San Francisco, Director of Salary Savings Sales for the U.S. and Canada, Branch Manager for the State of New Mexico, and General Agent in San Diego County.

His writing includes a number of magazine and newspaper articles about the Korean War and life insurance sales. His interest in California history and his travels and residency in the state created a dream to write a book about the little known historical events of early California.

Tom and Dolores, his wife of thirty years, live in Escondido, California.

Table of Contents

Cover vi

Dedication iii

Preface viii

The Spanish Period (1500 - 1821)

1. In the Beginning There was Nothing 1
2. Putting the Lid on California 7
3. Mission Accomplished 15
4. Captain Hippolyte de Bouchard 23
5. Manifest Destiny 28

The Mexican Period (1821 - 1848)

6. San Salvador Island 31
7. Fort Ross 33
8. Captain John Augustus Sutter 39
9. Land—Water—Sun 42
10. Thomas Larkin 52
11. Fort Catesby 57
12. Lieutenant Archibald Gillespie 60
13. Mountain Dolphins 64
14. Pre-Marshall Gold 71
15. General Stephen Watts Kearny 78
16. The War in the Baja 90

The American Period (1848 - 1860+)

17. Six Flags over California 93
18. Minorities 103
19. James King of William 110
20. The Graveyard of Ships 119
21. El Presidente Was a Gringo 134
22. The Mexican Expedition 139
23. The Nicaraguan Expedition 145
24. Epilogue 151
25. Appendix 153

The Cover

There are a good number of seals playing on the shores and rocks along the California coastline, however, The Great Seal of the State of California is found many miles inland at the State Capital in Sacramento.

Major R. S. Garnett of the United States Army designed the Great Seal in 1848, a year before California was admitted to the Union. Very few changes have been made to it over the years and those have been primarily to how the bear is portrayed. The bear has been shown asleep, chasing its tail, standing up, lying down, and eating hay, grapes, pears, apples, and grain. The current Great Seal reflects the "final" changes that were made in 1937.

There are thirty-one stars shown above the motto "Eureka." California was the thirty-first state admitted to the union. The word EUREKA in mythology means, "I found it," a phrase supposedly uttered by the Greek philosopher, Archimedes, when he discovered a method for determining the purity of gold.

The seal shows a miner with pick, shovel, and mining cradle representing the discovery of gold. The sailing ships in the harbor symbolize commercial greatness—please note that one is a steamship with smoke pouring out of the funnel.

The mountainous area in the background represents the Sierra Nevada mountain range, while the island in the bay, which is thought by many to be Alcatraz, is actually Yerba Buena Island that now anchors the Bay Bridge connecting San Francisco with Oakland. The grizzly bear standing by Minerva, is a symbol of determination and fierceness, and represents the many forms of wildlife found in the state. The bear is also in honor of the "Bear Flaggers" that were important in California history.

Minerva, the Roman goddess of wisdom, represents the fact that California was admitted to the Union directly as a state, without having served time as a territory. In Roman mythology, Minerva sprang full-grown from the forehead of her father, Jupiter.

From a First Day Cover illustration by Fred Collins

Preface

The California Chamber of Commerce paints the state as a land of sunshine and white sandy beaches. But there are also many rugged cliffs, heavy fog cover, stormy seas, treacherous tides, powerful currents, and underwater hazards such as rocks and shoals. The early Spanish explorers were faced with all of these elements, known and unknown.

This book outlines a few of the little known events from California's history. It is not a history book, but rather a book about a short segment in the development of the state prior to 1860.

It has been claimed by many that San Francisco Bay is one of the world's most beautiful harbors, but why did it take over two hundred years after the discovery of California for Spanish and English sailing ships to finally enter the Golden Gate? In fact it was not sailors that first saw this excellent anchorage, but rather Spanish soldiers on a land expedition that had traveled north from San Diego.

There is a story of a pirate with a black-hulled sailing vessel that left Argentina, sailed across the Atlantic, Indian, and Pacific Oceans, finally reached California and immediately began to burn and loot the capital.

History books tell how gold was discovered on one sunny Sunday morning in January, 1848, but knowledgeable people knew about gold deposits many years before. Both the American and Mexican governments had tried to keep it a secret.

A United States Marine officer pretended to be a crippled Cuban businessman on his way to China while, in fact, he was an American spy traversing Mexico. He was attempting to coordinate military action in California while serving as the personal messenger of the American president.

There is a story about General Kearny, who led an American army westward only to be defeated by a handful of Mexican caballeros at the Battle of San Pasqual. The general and his men were surrounded for several days and resorted to eating their mules before being rescued by U.S. Navy sailors and Marines from San Diego.

These are only a few of the exciting events that took place in early

California in what was then a far-off and relatively silent part of the world. These stories and many others will be told in the pages of this book. Events are never quite as portrayed in the official history books, and this volume is intended to give some background, color, and alternative interpretation to the events that shaped California's history.

Acknowledgements

The author gratefully acknowledges the contributions of other historians and authors who have contributed their insights to the history of California. Particularly important are the curators of the many public and private museums and libraries whose care and preservation of historical documents, implements, and records are essential to obtaining accurate accounts of events of the near and distant past.

—Chapter One—

IN THE BEGINNING THERE WAS NOTHING!

Nothing but sand, rocks, cactus, sagebrush, dirt, rattlesnakes, and very little water. Most of the area which we know today as Southern California, is semi-arid, which means it's as close to being a desert as you can get. The definition of desert means receiving less than ten inches of rainfall per year, which is generally true in the Southern California region and the Baja. Northern California land receives considerably more rain.

Away from the coastal beaches, but not yet to the Sierra Mountains, much of California's landscape consists of gentle hills and valleys.

For millions of years, this land lay in the hot boiling sun during daylight, with near freezing nights. The first visitors which left their footprints on this land were strange looking animals with strange names that we refer to as dinosaurs. Eons later came the Indians who tried to survive from day-to-day in this harsh, barren land.

In the years after the birth of Christ, when Europe and Asia were the centers of the civilized world, California lay dormant and barren, except for a few Indian tribes. It was not discovered by the Europeans until the late 15th century.

The first Spanish explorers thought that California from the Oregon border down to Cabo San Lucas was an island. It was only after an expedition in the Gulf of California (also known as the Sea of Cortez) that the Baja was found to be a peninsula. Sailing north in the gulf, the explorers reached the mouth of the Colorado River only to find that they had to make a U-turn and sail south again.

The land area of the Baja is about one-third the area of American California. The peninsula is about the same length as the state of

California. The Pacific coastline is about 1,000 miles long, and the eastern coast (Gulf of California) somewhat shorter. The Baja is twice the length of Florida, and is 100 miles longer than Italy. Even though very mountainous, most of this arid area is considered desert, as the only moisture comes from dense fogs, or damp winds from the Pacific, or an occasional rain from a hurricane. The highest point in Baja is Picacho del Diablo (Devils Peak), rising 10,154 feet from sea level. Often the range is snow-capped from October to May and can be seen from mainland Mexico 140 miles to the east.

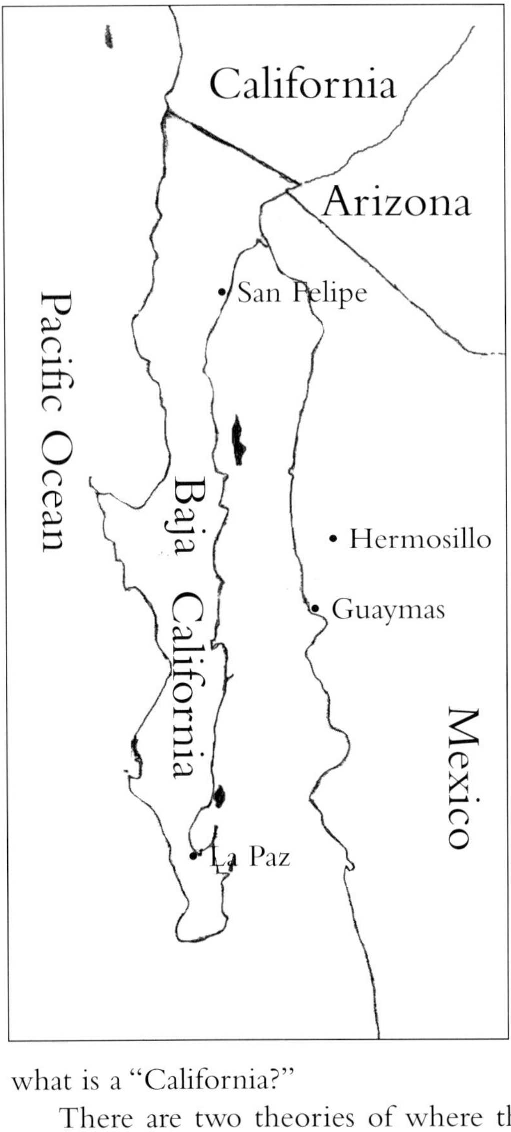

Where did the name California came from? Most names of cities, towns, villages, and hamlets of America came from the Indian, Spanish, French, or English languages, or took the names of great battles, or great men in history. Some were named from a description of the area, such as Hot Springs. But what is a "California?"

There are two theories of where the name California came from. Both involve the Baja. Just about every history book on California will mention the medieval romance novel called, "Las Sergas Esplandian" (The Exploits of Esplandian). The story tells about an island near the Indies that was peopled by large black women with beautiful and robust bodies, spirited courage and great strength. There were no men on this island, and the women would only invite those males of a neighboring area, to "come over and party" once a year. This mythical race of women warriors was ruled by a queen called CALIFIA. Their weapons were made from gold, as there was no other metal on the island.

The Spanish Conquistadores, of course, were searching for gold. They were also looking for a passage to the Indies. And third, but not necessarily in this order, they would welcome the company of women after being at sea for months at a time, and away from home several years. The great river found in South America, the Amazon, was named after the women they found there. And when the explorers found a village of beautiful Indian females and no men at what we now call La Paz, Baja, California, they named this newly found "island" after Queen Califia. Over time the name evolved into California. There must be some truth to this theory, because most history books retell the same story.

The second theory, which may be more plausible, uses the Latin words *callida fornax*, which mean "hot furnace." Combining the two words, one can see how the name California developed. When old Cortez stepped ashore one hot summer day in the Baja, he wiped his brow, and said, "Wow, it's like an oven here!" He marked his charts naming the bay, Callida Fornax, which some later explorers may have interpreted as the name of the region.

Several oddities within the animal kingdom occur in the Baja—rattlesnakes without any rattles. These can be found on San Pedro Island in the Gulf of California. There are jackrabbits with sleek black fur, which must be easy to hunt as they scurry amongst the cactus. There are also bats that catch and eat fish; two-foot-long Chuckwalla lizards that store so much water in their bodies that they gurgle when they walk. When these lizards can't find fresh water, which is most of the time, they drink salt water and have a built-in desalination plant that allow them to survive.

Whichever way the name came about, the Spanish felt they were on a large island surrounded by water. Much of California went unexplored with only the coastal plains being of interest to the Spanish sea captains and missionaries. Inland, some exploration was conducted in the coastal mountain ranges, but little was known about the vast valleys to the east until Juan Bautista Anza tackled the job on his trek from Yuma to Los Angeles in 1774. Little thought was given to the High Sierra Mountains that touched the sky east of the valley, and it would be a long time before knowledge of the desert beyond the Sierras was obtained.

> It is interesting to speculate what would have happened if, after the war with Mexico, the Baja would have become part of the United States. Just think what American land developers could have done with this virgin land parcel over the past 150 years or so! Or maybe it's just as well to leave the peninsula in the undeveloped stage. Where else could our off-road racers hold the Baja 1,000 mile race? More about the Baja later.

Today's California Chamber of Commerce may lead one to believe that wide and beautiful white beaches, with bright sunny skies, are typical throughout the State, but they are not representative of the entire coast. There are many miles of coast that are rugged cliffs, with pounding surf, tidal swirls, and currents that can dash boats onto uncharted rocks. Add to these conditions heavy fogs that hug the coast during summer months, with treacherous storms and high winds during the winter and a picture emerges of the California coast that is far from docile.

In the beginning, sailing ships from the Atlantic had to round Cape Horn at the tip of South America, then head north to Mexico and California. It was good sailing until they hit the Equator, where heavy winds and currents from the north forced the ships westward, usually as far as the Sandwich Islands (Hawaii), where the prevailing winds would permit a northward course. Catching the eastward Japanese current would then carry the ship to the California coast, somewhere between Mendocino and Monterey.

Spanish sailing masters had to be very careful when exploring the California coast. Without radar, sonar, or accurate maps, one mistake could not only result in the loss of the ship, but also cost the lives of the crew. The Golden Gate and the San Francisco Bay, are both shrouded in fog for most days during the year. Sir Francis Drake sailed right past one of the world's best harbors in 1579. Sebastian Vizcaino did the same thing in 1603. It wasn't until November 1769 that San Francisco was discovered—and then only by a soldier from land overlooking the bay! These dates are amazing! Almost 200 years elapsed from the time Spanish ships first sailed up and down the coast until one of the largest, best protected bays in the western hemisphere was discovered. In chapter two we will learn more about the exploration of this extensive and (then) barren coastline.

Cover illustration, The Call to California, *Union-Tribune Publishing Co.*

Satellite photo of the San Francisco Bay on a rare, uncloudy day. The large, protected bay provides one of the best natural harbors on the west coast, but it went undiscovered by early explorers because of the normally heavy fog conditions and the treacherous tidal ebbs and flows around the entrance to the harbor.

(NASA photo)

—Chapter Two—

PUTTING THE LID ON CALIFORNIA

The first Spanish exploration of California was only by sea along the fog bound coastline, which partly explains why it took more than 200 years for the San Francisco Bay to be discovered. After the death of Cabrillo, in 1543, Bartolome Ferrolo took command of the fleet and sailed northward to the Farallones Islands. He was only twenty-three miles away from the entrance to one of the greatest harbors of the world, but it was shrouded in fog. In 1579, Sir Francis Drake almost had the honor of the discovery, but again, sailed right on by due to the horrendous tides, currents, and, again, the heavy fog. Captain Sebastian Vizcaino came to the Farallones in 1602, but like the others before him, failed to travel the twenty-three miles for the discovery of several centuries.

Let's take a moment to analyze the problem of how Mother Nature frustrated the quest of experienced sailors to chart the coastline and find the entrance to the San Francisco Bay. First, and foremost, is the combination of tides, currents, and winds from the Pacific Ocean and the outflow of a large and powerful river we now know as the Sacramento. San Francisco Bay is the drainage basin for many rivers carrying the swollen snowmelt waters of the Sierra Nevada. During the spring the flood stage of these frigid waters creates a dense fog throughout the region. In addition, a wall of water called a tidal bore, builds up on the ebb tide that is hard to overcome for a sailing ship without strong winds to push it along. Add these conditions to being in uncharted waters, and a timid sailor or two will be found! The charts made by Ferrolo in 1543, and Vizcaino in 1602, showed the Farallones Islands, but did other dangers lurk in the fog? A good ship captain would give this area of coastline a wide berth. Even after the discovery of San Francisco Bay, sailing ships found it very difficult to enter, sometimes taking two or three days waiting for the right tide and current conditions. It was only after the invention of the steamship that headway could be made against these tidal conditions.

A European first saw San Francisco Bay in 1769, but he was not a sailor. Sergeant Ortega, a soldier with the Portola expedition, was amazed when he crested a hill and looked out over the vast expanse of water before him. The expedition had left Monterey several days before, making trail to Bodega Bay, which lay north of what is today the Golden Gate Bridge. Portola never made Bodega, as he could find no way around this large inlet and body of water to the east.

How did the old sailing ships make it all the way up the river to Sacramento during the gold rush? They did it the old fashioned way. First and foremost, the Sacramento River was then, and is today, a deep water ship channel. By using the sails and tacking as far up the river as possible, the ship would drop both forward anchors. A long boat would take one anchor up river to the end of its chain and drop it—the ship's crew would then pull up the other anchor, and winch it up river to where the other hook was set. This exercise would be repeated many times before the thirsty crew reached their objective of a grog shop in Sacramento. Coming down river was a 'breeze'—all that was required was to ride the current, steer the boat, and keep an eye peeled for sandbars. Sacramento was noted for its bars during the gold rush, both in the river, and on land!

Now let's find out a little about Don Gaspar de Portola, and his partner, Father Junipero Serra. During January of 1768, the Minister of State of Spain informed the Viceroy of Mexico that the Russians were making overtures towards California. The Viceroy issued orders for the immediate occupation of California by the traditional Spanish methods of civilizing the Indians and converting them to Christianity through the mission system.

The lower part of Baja, California from Cape San Lucas northward to La Paz and Loreto had been occupied by the Spanish for over seventy years—now it was time, "to put the lid on the rest of this vast territory." The Governor of the Baja was Don Gaspar de Portola, and he was instructed to send several ships north to Monterey, while he, personally, would lead a land exploration; first to San Diego, then on to Monterey. Father Junipero Serra would join the land expedition, with instructions to create mission churches throughout northern Baja and California. The Viceroy of Mexico wanted, "to make a ladder of missions all the way to Monterey." A brief description of the land and coast will help develop a better understanding of the project Portola was about to begin.

The California seacoast extends 1,264 miles, spanning nearly ten degrees of latitude—transfer this to the Atlantic coast and the shoreline would extend from Boston to Charleston, South Carolina. The land area of the state is greater than eighty-five individual world nations. California now houses more people than 114 sovereign countries, and is the third largest of fifty states. Mt. Whitney is the highest point in the continental United States at 14,496 feet. A few short miles away, is Death Valley with the lowest point in the U.S. at 279.6 feet below sea level. At the time of the Spanish exploration there were approximately 250,000 Indians trying to survive in this harsh land, more than enough to wipe out the handful of white men invading this territory. Fortunately for Portola the majority of Indians were very friendly, as we will see as we travel along with him and Fr. Serra on the trek northward.

The first step in putting the lid on California was to send two ships northward to establish a mission at San Diego, then on to Monterey to do the same. Because of his poor health and advanced age (fifty-five), Father Junipero Serra was forbidden to go by sea—instead he would make the 1,000 mile plus journey on the back of a mule. Father Juan Crespi, a much younger man than Serra, would also accompany the land expedition. He was responsible for keeping the official daily diary.

The two ships, the SAN CARLOS and the SAN ANTONIO, left La Paz during the winter months, and immediately ran into trouble with severe Pacific Ocean storms. Adverse winds, northern squalls, and sometimes even calm weather, hampered the progress of the ships that had left several weeks apart. Scurvy took its toll, and death came to several soldiers and crew as everyone aboard ship was subsisting on biscuits and dried salt beef. Aboard the SAN CARLOS, it didn't help matters when the fresh water caskets in the hold began leaking from the constant pitching of the ship in the heavy seas.

The trip by sea had been cruel for both ships, however, the SAN ANTONIO reached San Diego well ahead of the SAN CARLOS which had missed the entrance in a thick fog. Sailing northward, the ship found itself amongst the Channel Islands and had to turn back towards San Diego. After being at sea for 110 days, the SAN CARLOS finally came abreast of the entrance to San Diego, where the crew could see the SAN ANTONIO lying at anchor in the bay. However, it would be several more days before they could join the other ship, as the wind had died, and they had become entangled in a thick kelp bed.

The journey by land had also been cruel—none of the soldiers or missionaries had scurvy—but they had to fight the desert-like conditions, mountainous terrain, and canyons, some of which were 1,200 feet deep.

The expedition consisted of several hundred mules and horses and about 130 people: soldiers, missionaries, and Indian porters. The scarcity of water and lack of grass was the biggest problem the land expedition confronted in the barren country. The further north it traveled, the terrain would change from arid to semi-arid. Trees and game became more prevalent, as well as grass and watering holes. Soon the hills rose higher and higher, streams turned into small rivers with wild flowers blooming in the meadows. Jagged rocks and thorns all but disappeared and were replaced by a country green and rich in vegetation. The country was good and the Indians the expedition encountered were tall and robust and more curious than dangerous.

Spanish expedition trail

On May 13, 1769 a small hill was crested and in the distance lay a large bay on the coast of the Pacific Ocean. Through the afternoon haze, two ships could be seen lying at anchor. The long journey through the Baja to San Diego had finally been completed. Now they must rest and gain strength for an equally difficult trek to Monterey.

On July 14, 1769 Portola was again ready to resume the northward march. Well supplied from the ships, he started out with 163 mules and seventy-four people. The soldiers wore heavy leather jackets to protect against the possibility of Indian arrows. Portola wrote in his journal, "...their offensive arms are the lance, which they handle adroitly on horseback, the broadsword and the short musket, which they carry securely fastened in its case. They are men of great fortitude and patience...and we do not hesitate to say that they are the best horsemen in the world."

Passing through many Indian villages, along what is now northern San Diego County, the explorers were welcomed with open arms by the Diegueños Indians, a branch of the Yuman Tribe. After the harsh terrain of the Baja, this new land of the north was described as, "Mellow and fragrant—with many trees, wild fruit, and flowers everywhere." It reminded the men of the landscape found in Spain.

While passing through what is now Orange County, the Channel Islands of San Clemente and Catalina could be seen offshore. One mystery was presented to the explorers that to this day is unexplained. A number of the Indians in this area had lighter skin, with fair-hair, and even some of the children were blond with blue eyes. These people may have been the offspring of ship-wrecked European sailors, but no evidence of this fact has surfaced.

In order to ensure a supply of water, Portola's group turned inland to follow the foothills of the nearby mountains. East of present day Anaheim, they came to the Santa Ana River, and even though it was July and the middle of the dry season, the river was a rushing torrent.

Many earthquakes were experienced during the next few days, and the explorers gave the area a name, which needs no interpretation: "Rio de los Temblores."

Continuing northward, Portola and his group came to the San Gabriel River, which he immediately recognized as an excellent site for a mission. The earthquakes continued with violent and increased intensity—sometimes six or seven major quakes per day. Great herds of antelopes were sighted and soldiers immediately gave chase to augment the food supply.

The expedition next came to the Los Angeles River, which they forded without too much difficulty. Continuing along the base of the Santa Monica Mountains, they encountered many more earthquakes. Believing there must be active volcanoes in the area, scouts were sent ahead, and the following journal entry made:

"When this area was scouted, the Captain told me that about a half league to the west of here, in a ravine, they had come across about forty springs of tar, or pitch, boiling up out of the ground molten, and the water runs to one side and the pitch to another; they saw great swamps of this pitch, enough they said to caulk many vessels."

What the scouts had seen was most likely the present day La Brea Tar Pits, or perhaps the tar springs that run underneath the current Hollywood Freeway. It is interesting to note that beneath the hooves of the explorers' horses was oil, a wealth undreamed of by the Spanish Empire. In fact, the oil, when extracted, would be worth more than all the gold taken in the conquest of Mexico and Peru.

Rather than continuing northward after discovering and exploring the San Fernando Valley, Portola was convinced by the local Indians to cross the Santa Monica Mountains to what is now Santa Barbara. Here they found what they called, "The Canoe People." These Indians commuted to the Channel Islands in great canoes, some up to twenty-five feet long, all caulked with "asphaltium." This black gooey substance was plentiful in the area, seeping freely out of cracks in the ground and along the beach.

Leaving Santa Barbara far behind, the next few days were uneventful for Portola and his group, except they had entered grizzly bear country. Tracks from the huge animals were found everywhere, so one day the soldiers formed a hunting party and killed a very large specimen (375 pounds) near Pismo Beach.

Continuing northward, Portola missed a route that would have led them easily to Monterey. The expedition could have followed the San Luis Obispo Creek to the northwest (present day Highway 101) up the Salinas Valley, but instead Portola chose the rocky and mountainous coast (present day Highway 1). This route resulted in the most hazardous part of the journey: high mountains and foul weather.

La Brea Tar Pits

Several more days passed without seeing any evidence of Indians, or even the natives' villages. Many "troops" of grizzly bears were seen in the canyons west of San Luis Obispo. These sightings were akin to the western frontiersmen's sightings of the vast buffalo herds of the great plains. Portola and his men became entirely lost in the vast high mountains and deep canyons of the region. They knew it was only a short distance to their

The Canoe People; illustration courtesy of The Call to California, *Union-Tribune Publishing Co.*

destination, but fate would dictate six more discouraging weeks due to the rugged terrain and unfavorable weather.

The date was September 30, 1769 and the expedition had been making trail eighty days since leaving San Diego. By their calculations, they had traveled 411 miles. The actual distance between San Diego and Monterey, by Highway 101, is 452 miles. The men were exhausted, half of them were sick with scurvy—more and more time was lost resting the animals and men. Scouting parties only found more mountains and rivers to cross—still no Monterey. The days passed wandering through strange looking and very large red trees—never seen before by these men experienced in world travel. On October 18, they left these redwoods behind, and entered hilly land with many rivers, streams, and ravines. Hard luck continued the next day as they passed alongside a deep ravine, the mule that carried the kettle fell over the side to his death. They named the area, "Barranco de la Olla," meaning Kettle Ravine. Added to the mis-

It is interesting that with all the modern day news articles and talk of oil spills and illegal pumping of ship bilges ruining our beaches, that the white sands of California have seen their share of environmental ruin for millions of years. I remember as a boy growing up in the surf and sand of Southern California, how black my feet, especially the toes, and legs became, when running or swimming through great blobs of floating tar. My Dad would keep a large can of kerosene in the garage for me to wash off with upon returning from the beach each summer day. Not all of our entire environmental hazard is caused by modern man—sometimes Mother Nature takes her toll as well.

ery of the trail, was the start of wet season. Cold rains drenched man and animal alike—they must reach Monterey soon or all would perish.

On November 1, the decision was made to return to San Diego, but before reversing their steps, food supplies were needed. Sergeant Ortega and his scouts went forth after deer, and upon cresting a large hill, the hunting party looked down upon a great estuary, which proved later to be San Francisco Bay.

The journey north had taken four months. The return to San Diego, by a more direct route through the Central Valley, was accomplished in less than two and a half months. And Monterey still hadn't been reached by land. It would be another year before that was accomplished.

What was ironic about the first trip, is the fact that they had passed through the Monterey area without recognizing it. Until then Monterey had only been seen by ship captains and their crews. During nice weather, the sea approach made Monterey Bay look ideal as a safe anchorage. From the land approach, it was described in Portola's journal as being a half moon lagoon, open to the ravages of the sea. When Portola and his men passed through the area, heavy winter storms had started, with crashing surf and driving rains—hardly a safe haven for ships and sailors!

With the establishment of missions along the interior route to San Francisco, the lid was finally put on California—it was not until the discovery of gold, seventy-nine years later, that the lid would be completely blown off!

The next chapter will discuss the importance of the California missions and the presidios.

The California grizzly bear is now extinct, but there were plenty of them around in the early days of exploration. The much smaller brown, and also black bears, now roam various parts of the California countryside. These bears are not as mean as the grizzly, but you still want to give them a wide berth.

Fred Collins cachet #H2002

—Chapter Three—

MISSION ACCOMPLISHED

The Pacific Ocean, often referred to as the "Spanish Lake," forms the western coastline of the state of California. In the 1700s sailing vessels from England and France were threatening Spanish hegemony and Russia was making direct overtures towards Spanish California. In response, Spain decided that a show of force was required in order to maintain Spanish control and influence and to keep foreigners out of the territory. Governor Portola was ordered by his superiors in Mexico City to establish population centers centered around Catholic missions and presidios throughout California. A presidio is the Spanish word for a frontier military fort.

Which was the more important factor in establishing the Spanish claim to California; building the missions or building the presidios?

Modern day California is alive with references to the old Spanish missions. Every city, town, village, and even wide spots in the roads, seem to have names or logos that relate to the early California missions. From taco stands to railroad stations architectural design is in keeping with the adobe structures built by Spanish explorers. The word "mission" is used heavily in advertising both products from and places within the state. The "original" missions themselves have all been refurbished during the last century and now constitute a major attraction, bringing residents and tourists alike along the highways of the state to visit the "ladder of missions."

The Missions

The primary objective of the "ladder of missions" which extended north from San Diego to Sonoma was not only for the conversion of the Native American tribes to Christianity, but also to train the Indians for life in a European colonial society. The converts, referred to as "neophytes," were taught not only the new language and religion, but they were also trained in domestic skills like weaving, tanning of hides, brick-

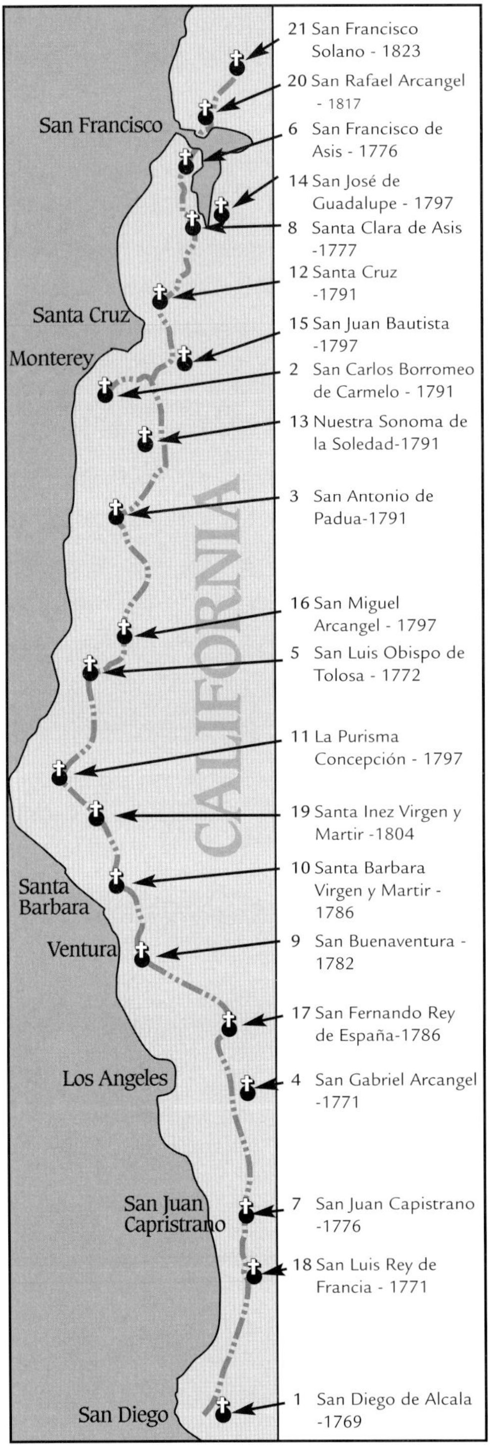

making, and the care and raising of cattle and horses. When the learning phase was completed, the "graduates" were expected to leave the mission and move to ranchos (small ranches) or to pueblos (small towns outside the mission walls).

Then, as now, earthquakes were a factor in the colonization of California. Missions were built primarily from adobe (mud and straw bricks baked in the sun). They did not use reinforced steel set in cement or even wooden structures as are built today, so when the big 1812 earthquake hit southern California, the missions were devastated. Many were relocated several miles from the original site before being rebuilt.

Heavy winter rains also took their toll on the adobe structures, washing away or badly eroding the mud bricks. The Spaniards remembered that similarly constructed bricks at home in Spain were "kiln-fired" for fire retardation. When kiln firing was used for adobe bricks, the hardened surface was much more stable, thereby improving the structural integrity of the mission buildings. If only the "earthquake problem" could be solved so simply!

The missions, briefly described, are listed below in the order in which they were established. Most cities in which the missions are located are named after the mission.

#1 San Diego de Alcala July 16, 1769

San Diego is the first link in the "chain" that stretches 650 miles north along the El Camino Real, the royal road or Kings Highway. It was named for Saint Didacus of Alcala and is located on Presidio Hill in San Diego.

#2 San Carlos Borromeo de Carmelo June 3, 1770

This mission is considered the "most beautiful" of all the California missions. It was named for Saint Charles Borromeo and is located south of Carmel.

#3 San Antonio de Padua July 14, 1771

This mission lays claim to being the first gristmill in California. It was named for Saint Anthony and is located near Jolon in Monterey County.

San Carlos Borromeo de Carmelo from a Fred Collins First Day Cover

#4 San Gabriel Arcangel September 8, 1771

Known as the "Queen of the Missions," it was one of the most prosperous missions as well as being one of the most difficult to manage because it was on a heavily traveled immigrant east-to-west trail. Many weary travelers crowded the mission after their hot and dry crossing of the desert and unwelcome guests, including military detachments, were usually very disruptive to the missionaries and their Native American students. The mission was named for the Archangel Gabriel and is located in the city of San Gabriel.

#5 San Luis Obispo de Tolosa September 1, 1772
The halfway point, geographically, in the chain of missions. The mission was named for Saint Luis, Bishop of Toulouse and is located in the city of San Luis Obispo.

#6 San Francisco de Asis June 26, 1776
Better known as Mission Dolores, it is named for Saint Francis of Assisi and is located in San Francisco.

#7 San Juan Capistrano November 1, 1776
A small chapel (Serra's Church) built next to the mission is believed to be the oldest church in California. The mission is known as "the jewel of the missions" and is famous for the annual migration of the swallows. It was named for Saint John of Capistrano, Italy and is located in the small town of San Juan Capistrano.

San Juan Capistrano

#8 Santa Clara de Asis January 12, 1777
This was the first mission named for a woman, Saint Claire of Assisi, who was the founder of Poor Claire's order of nuns. It is located in the city of Santa Clara.

#9 San Buenaventura March 31, 1782
Originally planned as the third mission, the lack of military escorts because of problems in San Diego caused postponement of its construction for almost twelve years. It is named after Saint Bonaventure and is located in the city of Ventura.

#10 Santa Barbara December 4, 1786
Documents for the entire mission system can be found at this mission as well as sheet music of the late 1700s. It was named for Saint Barbara and is located in Santa Barbara.

#11 La Purisima Concepción December 8, 1787
The mission is named for the Immaculate Concepción of Mary the Most Pure and is located north of the town of Lompoc.

#12 Santa Cruz August 28, 1791
The mission is named for the Sacred Cross and is located in Santa Cruz, north of Monterey Bay.

#13 Nuestra Señora de la Soledad October 9, 1791
Located south of the town of Soledad, the mission is named for Our Lady of Solitude.

#14 San José July 11, 1797
This is the first mission built whose primary purpose was to shorten the distance between missions to one day of safe travel time. It was named for Saint Joseph and is located north of the city of San Jose.

#15 San Juan Bautista June 24, 1797
Thomas Doak, a sailor who had jumped ship and became the first anglo-American resident of California painted the interior of this mission. The colors Doak mixed were so durable that they continue to glow to this day. The mission of San Juan is also noted for being built directly on the San Andreas earthquake fault. It was named for John the Baptist and is located just north of Salinas in the town of San Juan Bautista.

#16 San Miguel Arcangel July 25, 1797
The mission is named for Saint Michael the Archangel and is located north of the city of Paso Robles.

#17 San Fernando Rey de España
September 8, 1797

When an old mission is shown in a motion picture, it is most likely to be this one because of its proximity to Hollywood. It is also the largest adobe structure in California. One of the earliest gold finds occurred on a neighboring land grant when the mission was secularized in the 1830s. It was named for Saint Ferdinand, King of Spain (1217-1252) and is located west of the city of San Fernando.

#18 San Luis Rey de Francia — June 13, 1798

Nicknamed "King of the Missions," at its peak occupation, the Native American population reached 2700 with the largest herd of livestock of all the missions: 50,000 cattle and sheep, 1300 goats, 300 pigs, and 2000 horses. The mission was named for Louis IX, King of France (1215-1270) and is located in the town of San Luis Rey.

#19 Santa Ines — September 17, 1804

This was the last mission to be built in southern California. It was named for Saint Agnes and is located in the town of Solvang.

#20 San Rafael Arcangel — December 14, 1817

Originally dedicated as an asistencia (a sub-mission) to Mission Dolores in San Francisco, it was given full mission status in 1822. The mission was named for Saint Raphael the Archangel, patron of good health. It is located north of San Francisco in the city of San Rafael.

#21 San Francisco Solano — July 4, 1823

It would shortly come under the control of General Mariano Vallejo and add its place in history as the location of the Bear Flag Revolt. It was named for Saint Francis Solano and is located twenty miles north of San Francisco in the town of Sonoma.

As the reader can determine from the founding dates above, twenty of the missions were built under Spanish rule; only one was built after the Mexican Revolution of 1821. The "mission of the missions" to convert the natives and build a population loyal to Catholic Spain (and, subsequently, Mexico), had been accomplished.

The Presidios

The function of the presidio was primarily defensive. A fort was to be established for every five or six missions in order to protect Spanish towns, friendly Indian villages, the land grants, and mining camps. For the twenty-one missions in the ladder, four presidios were built: San Diego, Monterey, San Francisco, and then, because of the distance between San Diego and Monterey, the distance was split almost equally and a presidio was established at Santa Barbara.

The soldiers of the presidios had a hard life. They had few supplies and poor pay. But a major problem developed when the politicians and military elite in Mexico City sent criminals and vagabonds from the jails of central Mexico to act as soldiers on the California frontier. The convict soldiers were rowdy, insolent, and immoral. This cheap labor austerity program backfired when the soldiers clashed with the missionaries over the treatment of Indian women and enslavement of Indian men.

Spanish presidio at Monterey, California; illustration from Pictorial History of California, *Doubleday, NY.*

The missionaries' most bitter complaint was the abuse of Indian women by the soldiers. There were no European or Mexican females in California prior to the 1800s. Additionally, the Spanish caste system discouraged marriages between soldiers and Indian women. And soldiers, unlike their missionary counterparts, did not take vows of celibacy. Father Serra begged the Viceroy not to turn California into a penal colony or place of exile for criminals who would mistreat the native population that he was trying to convert. He pleaded in his complaint to the Viceroy that "the Indians believe Spaniards were offspring of mules—seeing that mules were the only members of the female gender among us." Serra also pleaded that "mujeres blancos (white women) be sent to California in numbers at least equal to the number of male convict soldiers."

Not all the military men were rogues. Many soldiers retired from the service and intermarried with civilian families and they and their offspring became leaders in the land grant elite of California. In this way, the presidios had a lasting influence and social impact on the history of California and, it could be argued, that their influence was greater than that of the mission system.

With the establishment of both the missions and the presidios, the threat of invasion from the Pacific Ocean by the other European powers had been effectively thwarted. The Russians would soon retire to Alaska and England would concentrate their expansion efforts north of California.

But the guns of the presidios were pointed in the wrong direction. In only a few years the Argonauts from the east would begin a land invasion that neither the mission system nor the military might of Mexico would be able to stop. The seekers of the Golden Fleece would allow nothing—mountains, deserts, nor military power—to keep them from their manifest destiny.

But before a discussion of "manifest destiny" in chapter five, a little known episode in California history that involved several hundred pirates who invaded Monterey will be described in the next chapter.

—Chapter Four—

CAPTAIN HIPPOLYTE DE BOUCHARD
Argentine naval officer, privateer, and pirate

As the two Argentine marines left the ship, Bouchard informed them that his name was "Captain Bouchard, not 'Old Hippo'." They had been guilty of referring to the chief officer during a private conversation that was overheard by one of the crew and reported to the captain.

The marines were on their way by longboat to the desolate Isla del Muerto better known as Dead Man's Island. They had both received a twelve-lash flogging, and now faced the barren and waterless land that would be their home until they died from starvation and thirst. Isla del Muerto was one of the smaller islands that make up what is known as the Channel Islands, that lay just off the coast of Santa Barbara and run southward to Catalina, twenty miles west of San Pedro. The island was a barren plateau atop forty-foot cliffs. The water around the island rippled with *el gran tiburon*, in other words, sharks! The date was December 17, 1818. More on this later.

Captain Hippolyte de Bouchard was thirty-five years old and was born in St. Tropez, France. Moving to Buenos Aires, Argentina at an early age, he married and served in the Argentina navy. During the time of the country's struggle to be independent from Spain, Bouchard was given his own ship. As a privateer, he was authorized to attack and capture enemy ships in the name of the Argentina government. On July 9, 1817 he began an around-the-world voyage, knowing that the Pacific Ocean was considered a "Spanish Lake," and those pickings would be pretty good. Privateers, better known as pirates, did not owe allegiance to any one country, and Bouchard's mission was not one of exploration or the taking of territory. Only his hatred of the Spaniards dictated his choice of targets. Argentina, the country, was not a primary force in the world, but with the forty-two-gun frigate named ARGENTINA painted black, the Pacific became his oyster.

Sailing eastward across the Atlantic, the black frigate rounded Africa's Cape of Good Hope, then sailed on to Madagascar, Indonesia, and the Philippines, raiding Spanish ships and ports along the way. Now, Bouchard discovered that he had the same problem as Sir Francis Drake, who had sailed many years before; his decks had become too heavy with treasure. Captain Bouchard decided to stop over in the Sandwich Islands (now known as Hawaii) to unload and find crew replacements as 100 men had died from scurvy during the voyage.

Another Argentine ship named the SANTA ROSA, also a privateer, had arrived in Hawaii several weeks before, commanded by a man calling himself Captain Turner. Suspicions were aroused when the SANTA ROSA was offered to King Kamehameha at a very low price. Upon investigation, it was found that the crew had mutinied after rounding The Horn and the real captain had been put ashore on a desolate island.

Bouchard convinced King Kamehameha that he had written instructions from his homeland that the SANTA ROSA was to be under the command of Bouchard. These papers had been forged by Bouchard, but the King agreed. Several weeks were spent rounding up a crew for the SANTA ROSA, and adding to the crew of *la fragata negra*, the black frigate named ARGENTINA. All told, 350 cut-throats, thieves, and revolutionaries joined Bouchard for his raid against the coast of California. The crew was made up of Malays, Portuguese, Spaniards, Englishmen, Australians, and Sandwich Islanders (Hawaiians).

Earlier, a ship commanded by a Captain Gyselar, left Hawaii and had sailed for Santa Barbara where the locals were notified of Bouchard's plans. Warning was sent northward to Monterey, however, Governor Sola was not particularly concerned, but he did notify the presidio. After several weeks passed, and no pirates showed up, the fort went back to business as usual, a somnolent, lackadaisical routine. What they did not know was that Bouchard had sailed to the Russian port of Fort Ross, north of San Francisco, where he laid aboard supplies of fresh fruits and eggs. Upon leaving Fort Ross, the ARGENTINA and the SANTA ROSA, turned south towards Monterey and the hated Spaniards.

Just the sight of an all black frigate, bristling with gun ports was enough to scare just about anyone, but having two ships enter the Bay of Monterey together, meant real trouble. The problem was that the presidio only had forty soldiers; hardly enough to defend against a landing party of several hundred pirates. The following message was sent ashore to the presidio:

To the Commandant of the Port of Monterey

Dear Sir:

Since the King of Spain has declared bloody war on my country, Argentina, I am making a defense by waging war on land and sea and in every port King Ferdinand dares to call his own.

Therefore, having crossed the Pacific Ocean to this coast, I now desire the surrender of your city with all the furniture and other belongings of the king. If you do not do so, the city will be reduced to cinders, and also the other surrounding villages. It is within my power to bring about this destruction.

You may evade all the above spilling of blood by agreeing to my proposal. If so, I shall desist from what I say. Be good enough to reply to me as soon as possible.

May God keep you many years.

Signed,
Hippolyte de Bouchard
Aboard the Argentina.
Dated November 23, 1818.

Governor Sola sent an immediate reply, which in essence said, "Go to hell, we will defend this town to the last man, women, and child!" Then the fun began.

A two-hour exchange of cannon shots between the ships and the presidio did no damage to either side, but it had bought time for the town people to evacuate and escape to the countryside. When boat-load after boat-load of cutthroats came ashore setting up their cannons on a knoll overlooking the town, the presidio soldiers knew it was time for them to also evacuate to the countryside.

Governor Pablo Vicente de Sola, the last Spaniard to rule California, was not real happy with the soldiers sent to him from Mexico City. He referred to them as *cholos* and described them as "vicious, quarrelsome vagabonds, without religion, drunkards, gamblers, thieves, and *léperos*." It appears that these fine fellows could qualify to work for Bouchard, as pirates, if they decided to leave the army. The Governor kept the hard liquor under lock and key, but it didn't take the pirates long to find the grog supply. The more they drank, the louder they became. They stayed a full week in Monterey, looting, burning, and sacking every building and home. The Sandwich Island warriors, it has been said, came ashore completely naked, with spears, shields, and war paint. When they left, seven days later, they were attired in the finest Spanish clothing, obtained the old fashioned way. From the looks of their fancy dress (and yes, some did wear dresses) it must have been the Governor's own home that got raided before being burnt to the ground.

Some of the drunken pirates strayed away from the merriment, which was a big mistake. A group of *vaqueros* (cowboys) used their lassos on three of the pirates and dragged them south towards Santa Barbara. This caused 'Old Hippo' to become very mad (I had better watch what I call him). The pirates immediately loaded their ships and weighed anchor, but not before taking aboard two apparently willing Indian girls to brighten the voyage.

Hippolyte de Bouchard; illustration from Pictorial History of California, *Doubleday, NY.*

Three young schoolboys had witnessed the carnage of their town; Mariano Vallejo, Jose Castro, and Juan Alvarado. These native sons of California would in later years become the three most powerful men in the state.

Upon arrival, just north of Santa Barbara, Bouchard negotiated with the townspeople that he would not sack the town, if they in return would release his men that had been captured. Upon the return of these men, the two ships headed south towards the Baja and the hoped-for more lucrative Spanish treasures.

But first, there is the matter of the two Marines that needed to be flogged and sent ashore.

During the early exploration of California by sea, San Diego and San Francisco were found to be natural harbors. Monterey, San Pedro, and Santa Barbara were not classed as such, because their harbors were no more than large bays, open to the Pacific swells and storms. The Channel Islands, some larger than others, and some no more than rocky reefs, were numerous between Santa Barbara and San Pedro. Fog bound sailors had to keep their wits about them or else the crashing surf would doom both them and their ships. One of the smaller islands was just off what is known today as the Los Angeles and Long Beach harbors, both of which are man-made and not natural. This small island known as *Isla del Muerto*, or Dead Man's Island is no longer a navigational threat. It was shaved down to the waterline and became the base for large granite boulders now making up the breakwater of the outer harbor, or anchorage, at San Pedro. This breakwater is huge and extends nine miles; anchored at one end by the once famous Island of the Dead.

Treasure hunters have swarmed over the small island for years and have found numerous graves of people that had spent their last moments on earth without water or food, abandoned on this desolate desert island. It is unknown whether any treasure was ever found, but a number of artifacts were dug up, including boots and sabers of the conquistadores. It is not known whether the artifacts found included Argentine marine emblems, but it has been rumored that the two Indian girls from Monterey were also left on the island with the two marines, so at least they had company at the end. Who knows what fate fell on our friends, as 'Old Hippo' sailed south to other conquests, never to be heard from again.

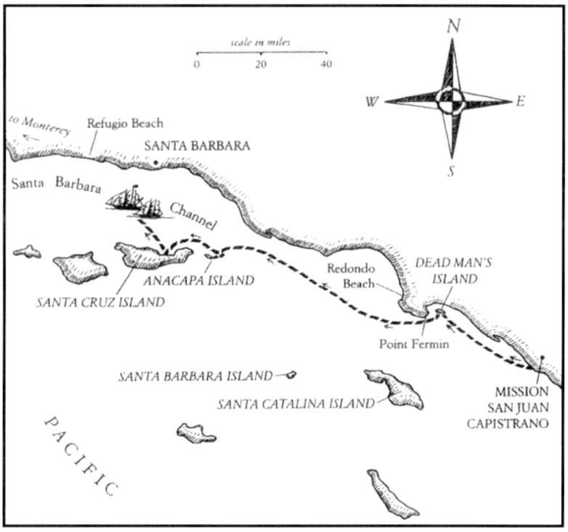

From an early California coastal map (California Historical Society)

—Chapter Five—

MANIFEST DESTINY

While the Spanish were setting up missions and presidios during the exploration of coastal California, 3,000 miles to the east a young nation was about to be born. At the successful conclusion of the Revolutionary War against England, the new Congress of the United States had many decisions to make. One topic concerned the formation of states and territories within the new nation. It was agreed that the "youngster" must learn to crawl before walking and must walk before running. Any thoughts of expansion into foreign lands bordering the new nation must come at a later date. Thus the idea of a "manifest destiny" was put on a back burner.

As the new nation grew towards adulthood, growing pains dictated expansion of its territories westward. One key factor during these early years was the Mexican Revolution that in 1821 resulted in the loss of influence by Spain in Mexico as well as in South and Central America. Spain's loss became the United States' gain, and the new nation became very greedy for new lands.

Northern Mexico, which included what would become the states of Arizona, Nevada, Utah, New Mexico, parts of Wyoming and Colorado, and both upper and lower California, were a vast wasteland consisting mainly of

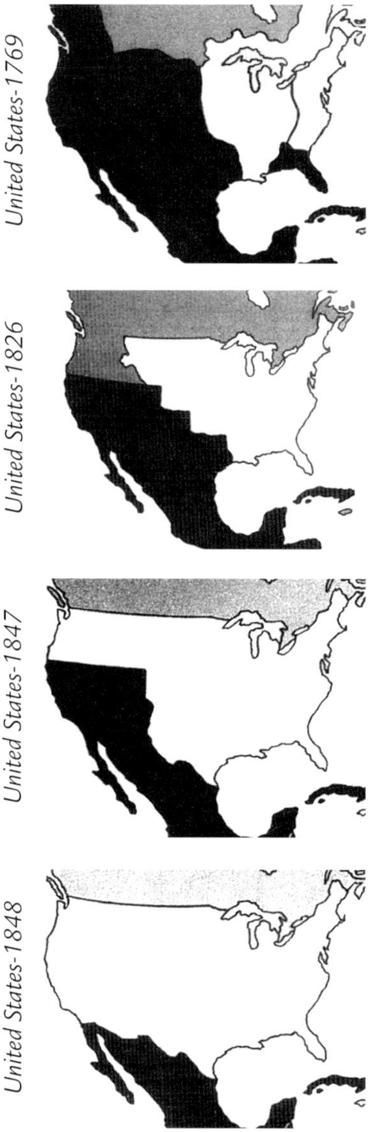

The territorial growth of the United States of America; illustrations from Pictorial History of California, *Doubleday, NY.*

deserts, high mountain ranges, dormant volcanoes and ancient sea-floors. The area was inhabited by tribes of native American Indians, some of whom were hostile. It was not worth a whole lot to the Mexican government because of the high cost of maintenance and defense. Perhaps the United States could diplomatically offer to purchase these territories in order to gain access to the Californias and the Pacific Ocean.

One problem the United States government faced was the low population density of Northern Mexico. American settlers would be needed to occupy the territory. What would be the incentive for people on the east coast to move west? (For this answer, see Chapter Fourteen, Pre-Marshall Gold.)

Another problem facing congress was the expansionist movements by European nations other than Spain. England was again saber rattling about control of the real estate north of Mexico's California (the states known today as Oregon and Washington.) The only thing keeping the British from moving into California was the United States superior naval fleet in the Pacific. The new nation had several squadrons of warships in position from Acapulco to northern California. The French had an eye on expansion into the new world, but had suffered setbacks both militarily and financially due to the losses by Napoleon. The Russians had well-established fur trading companies, but little military presence. Even though the European powers had ambitions, it was Mexico that was the real threat to American expansion. And it was Mexico, not knowing that it did so, that gave the United States the answer to the problem.

As the American population slowly moved westward, a number of settlers drifted into the Mexican territory known as Texas. The Mexican army tried to close the floodgates with no success. Soon, uprisings brought revolution by the new settlers who declared independence from both Mexico and the United States.

Mexico agreed to the independence, but only with the understanding that war would be declared if Texas was annexed to the United States. Several years later, application was made by Texas for statehood in the expanding union, war was declared, and the rest is history.

Meanwhile, life in California was good, but became even better as the Mexican army moved southward to join forces in defense of Mexico and Texas. The idea of manifest destiny was now firmly implanted in the culture of the rapidly expanding nation. In fact, as will be discussed in later chapters, some Americans wanted to carry the concept of manifest destiny to extremes by including ALL of Mexico and ALL of Central America.

—Chapter Six—

SAN SALVADOR ISLAND

Better known today as Santa Catalina, the island was first visited by Juan Rodriguez Cabrillo on October 7, 1542. The visit was duly noted in the logbook, and the island was officially named after Cabrillo's ship, SAN SALVADOR. Sixty years later, on the eve of St. Catherine's Day, November 24, 1602 the island was sighted by Sebastian Viscaino, and renamed Santa Catalina in honor of Saint Catherine.

Santa Catalina joins with two other islands, San Clemente and San Nicholas, to make up the Southern Channel Islands. Santa Cruz, Santa Rosa, and San Miguel make up the Northern Channel Islands. Archaeologists excavating artifacts have estimated that people had lived on these islands at least 7,000 years ago. But, the real claim to fame for Catalina's history is the part it played in the smuggling of manufactured goods, as well as for the harvest of sea lion and sea otter pelts.

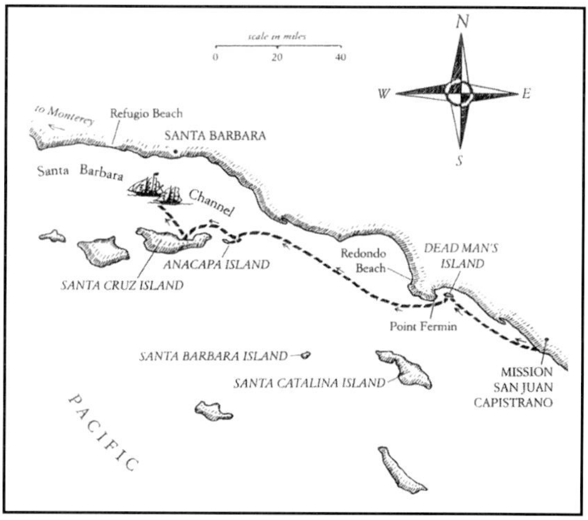

From an early California coastal map (California Historical Society)

Spain did not allow its colonies to trade with foreigners; however, there was no way Spain could police the elongated California coastline. The friars and townspeople would often trade leather hides and tallow and even pelts for manufactured goods, even though it was against the law. When Mexico became independent from Spain, in 1821, the Mexican government allowed trade with foreigners, but levied a high tariff on all imported goods. Ship captains would off-load half of their cargo in a secluded area of Catalina Island, then continue on to the customs house in Monterey where tax would be paid on the remaining cargo. A license would be issued for the ship to conduct legal trade up and down the

California coast—which they did, coming back to Catalina to replenish their stock. Again, it was impossible for the authorities to police this smuggling, so the tax was raised to 100% of the cargo value, thus netting the Mexicans approximately 50% on all goods (including those smuggled.)

Another little known colorful event occurred in Catalina many years after California joined the United States. The date was September 1, 1972. A large contingent of young people invaded the island and raised a large Mexican flag on the hill overlooking the town of Avalon. The invaders were dressed in military fashion, including brown berets. The citizens of Catalina at first thought it was the Mexican Army. David Sanchez, a former chairman of the Los Angeles Mayor's Youth Council, organized the Brown Berets in 1967. David and his followers did not seriously believe that they could regain Catalina for Mexico, in fact, they were unarmed. However, they did want to bring attention to the world that the Treaty of Guadalupe Hidalgo was in error by not including the Channel Islands off the coast of California as American territory. The Brown Beret occupation had continued for twenty-four days before the problems of Mexican-Americans, symbolized by their colonial status, were discussed.

The Treaty of Guadalupe Hidalgo, which ended the Mexican-American War, had been signed on February 2, 1848. The United States ratified the treaty on March 16, 1848 and Mexico ratified it on May 30, 1848. The President of the United States proclaimed and accepted the treaty on July 4, 1848. There are twenty-three articles in the treaty, of which number five (V), pertains to the boundaries of the two countries as follows:

"The Boundary line between the two Republics shall commence in the Gulf of Mexico, three leagues from land, opposite the mouth of the Rio Grande, otherwise called Rio Bravo del Norte...to a point on the coast of the Pacific Ocean, distant one marine league due south of the southernmost point of the Port of San Diego..."

It is interesting to note that one marine league equals three miles, thus a nine mile limit applied to the Atlantic coast, while no coastal territorial limit applied to the Pacific coast, except three miles south of the San Diego Bay. The Channel Islands were not named or described. Maybe David Sanchez and his band of Brown Berets had a valid point. Is the southernmost point of the San Diego Bay when the tide is in or when it is out?

—Chapter Seven—

FORT ROSS

What a strange name for something Russian—Ross almost sounds English! How did the fort come to be named? In Spanish it would be called *Fortaleza de los Rusos* (Fort of the Russians). Actually, the name, Russia, in Tsarist days, was *Rossiya*—the shortened version would be Ross. With that explanation of the name of the fort, what else is known about "Russian California"?

In 1841, Mexico City made one big mistake regarding the settlement north of San Francisco when it rejected the Russian offer to sell Fort Ross. The Mexicans felt that the Russians were trespassers, and had illegally entered Spanish California to build their fort in 1812. Why should Mexico City pay $30,000 to buy something the Russians were planning to abandon anyway?

The Russians had come to California from Alaska with no sword in hand, but rather as traders of furs and skins. The problem they were having in Alaska was lack of agriculture to feed the Russian hunters. American sea captains, when calling on Russian ports, would tell of mild climates in California with great abundance of wheat and cereals, plus an over-abundance of sea otters, seals, and other types of sea mammals.

Count Nikolai Petrovich Rezanov, Chamberlain of the Czar, left Sitka on the supply ship JUNO and sailed to San Francisco, where he met with Spanish officials. The Spanish, at first, rejected the Russian request to buy wheat, but later gave in when the Count met and fell in love with Concepción Arguello. Señorita Arguello happened to be the fifteen-year-old daughter of the San Francisco Commandant. During the whirlwind courtship of the señorita, the Count had sent the JUNO on a scouting mission of the California coastline. In a month, the ship would return to San Francisco with its hold full of sea otter skins.

Arrangements were soon being made for the marriage between the count and the señorita. After a brief honeymoon, the count decided to return to Russia alone, put his affairs in order, and return to San Francisco as a resident. Many months passed which turned into years. Finally word was received that the count had died while crossing Siberia. One wonders at the truth of this story. Perhaps his majesty was sipping vodka on the balcony of his chalet overlooking the Black Sea, and he had no visions of returning to the wild frontier of California.

In 1809 Ivan Kuskov, an officer with the Russian American Fur Company, sailed into Bodega Bay, which he found to be a safe and good harbor. The reader will remember from history books that Sir Francis Drake, 230 years before, had spent time in Bodega. Kuskov would return in 1812 and build a settlement eighteen miles north of Bodega, which he named Fort Ross. This land above San Francisco was still a primitive wilderness, the greater part of the area occupied only by bands of roving Indians.

The Spanish had never given their permission for Russia to settle the area, and upon hearing the news, immediately demanded the Russians leave. This order, of course, was ignored because Spain had no way of evicting the newcomers, which by now numbered about 400 people.

From 1812 until Russian withdrawal from California in 1842, it was not just a fort with cannons, but a regular town. It included windmills, watermills, orchards, crops, cattle, sheep, and even a shipyard. There were over fifty buildings including a carpenter shop, cooper shop, tannery, bakery, flour mill, dairy house, barns, stockhouses, boathouses, and living quarters. The fort itself was well defended by forty French brass cannons, which had been captured from Napoleon's army when retreating from Moscow.

Mountain howitzer at Fort Ross

In 1821, Spain lost control of its New World conquests, and now Mexico was concerned with the Russian presence in California. It was felt that any expansion eastward by the Russians would be detrimental to the Mexican territory. The need for level land, better weather, and fertile valleys would be high on the Russian agenda. Mexico City was still sore about Russia refusing to recognize Mexican independence from Spain.

General Mariano Guadalupe Vallejo, a native Californian from Monterey, was asked to set up a buffer zone against any eastern expansion by the Russians. Surveying the area, Vallejo set up his headquarters at Sonoma, and placed a colony at both Petaluma and Santa Rosa. It was like a game of chess, with the Russians having outposts of Aleut hunters on the Farallones Islands, twenty miles off the entrance to San Francisco Bay, and as far south as Catalina Island off of Los Angeles. Vallejo's settlements now became a checkmate to Russian expansion into the fertile valleys east of Fort Ross.

Russia had two objectives in settling California. One was the agricultural supplies needed for the Alaska operation, and second was the furs and skins that would help pay expenses. In 1812, there had been a record 40,000 skins taken—in 1820, less than 4,000 had been the harvest. The Russian emperor had decided to leave Fort Ross in 1838 because a secret arrangement had been made with the Hudson Bay Company to furnish food from Oregon and Washington to the Russian operations in Alaska. Now all they needed was a sucker to come along and buy Fort Ross. His name was John Augustus Sutter and he arrived the next year. But the Russians found out the hard way that old John was not the sucker they thought he was.

The Russians, as well as the politicians in Mexico City, were about to make one of the biggest mistakes in history. John Sutter, travelling to Monterey by way of the Sandwich Islands and Alaska, arrived at Fort Ross with his letters of introduction from the Russian American Fur Company. After being wined and dined, the Russians offered Sutter a deal he could hardly turn down. All the facilities of the fort, including livestock, crops, and several boats, for $50,000 cash. Sutter, of course, was not a man of wealth. He had always operated on the basis of credit. In turning the deal down, Sutter explained that he wanted to settle in a fertile valley close to a major river, and he hadn't met with the Mexican authorities yet to get approval to enter the country. Sutter also questioned the land title since the Russians had paid only a few strings of beads to the Indians for possession. In the back of Sutter's mind is what he had learned during his travels to Santa Fe about the mineral wealth of California. He could hardly become rich from salt water that stretched to the horizon from the front door of Fort Ross. Now maybe if the Russians were to offer an easy payment plan, he might reconsider the offer. But first he must visit Monterey.

The Russians contacted General Vallejo, Comandante of the North, and requested his approval for a sale of the facilities to an individual European, without naming Sutter. Vallejo responded, by saying that the Government of the Nation should have first right of purchase, and that he would send the information to Mexico City.

Meanwhile, on July 3, 1839, Sutter arrived at Monterey with his letters of introduction. Sutter had a winning personality, along with the ability to not only speak Spanish and English, but also French and German fluently. Governor Alvarado was overwhelmed with his guest, and gave Sutter permission to start a colony of settlers near the mountains to the east. Alvarado would also grant Sutter Mexican citizenship, and would allow one year to grant full title to any land Sutter might choose.

Upon returning to San Francisco, Sutter and his party immediately started up-river towards what would be their new home. With a boatload of supplies that he had brought from the Sandwich Islands, Sutter had also recruited eight male Kanakas, two female Wahines (Hawaiians, one of whom was Sutter's mistress), and three white men.

Back at Sonoma, Vallejo was giving a lot of thought about the Russian offer that he had sent on to Mexico City. Even if approval was not granted, maybe he could swing the purchase, which would allow him to open up the coastal territory for the Mexican nation. Not knowing how long it would take for a response (remember, they didn't have FAX machines in those days), Vallejo decided to open up negotiations for Fort Ross on his own behalf.

By now the Russians were getting a little fed up with the time lapse and wanted to get moving back to Alaska. They told Vallejo the deal was his as an individual for $30,000. Vallejo made a counter offer for $9,000, as all he wanted was the livestock, which consisted of 1,700 oxen and cows, 940 horses and mules, and 900 sheep. The Russians rejected this low-ball offer.

Meanwhile, word was finally received from Mexico City stating that the Russians had paid only a few beads for the land, which was not owned by the Indians in the first place, and that the equipment should be left without charge to the Mexicans, upon Russia vacating the premises. The Russians were amazed at this attitude, and declared that they would burn the facilities to the ground before leaving anything for Mexican use.

Contact was again made with Sutter, who by now had completed the first stage of building his fort on the confluence of the American and Sacramento Rivers. Sutter responded to the Russians that all he was interested in was the livestock.

The Russians, now fairly disgusted with the whole deal, threw up their hands and told Sutter he could have the whole ball of wax, including the Bodega Bay colony and the 20-ton schooner, CONSTANTINE, plus several other ships, for $30,000. All that was needed to put the sale to bed was $2,000 down with the $30,000 paid in four yearly installments of $7,500 each. Sutter would need to use his New Helvetia Fort property as collateral. "Not a bad deal," Sutter told himself, then asked the Russians if the installments "could be made in goods and produce, rather than cash?" The property deed was signed on December 13, 1841.

It would take Sutter two years to salvage Fort Ross, which was 125 miles from New Helvetia. First he moved 2,000 cattle, 100 of which drowned crossing the Sacramento River. Sutter's words were, "Most of them we salvaged downstream for their hides"—known at the time as "California bank notes." Next, he stripped the buildings for lumber, transported the 40-brass French cannons, and sent his employee, John Bidwell, to act as on-site manager of Fort Ross. Sutter then leased the land to another employee, which caused the Mexican authorities to become quite upset, as Sutter did not have title for the land.

Russian ships would call on Sutter once a year for the installments, which he never paid. The ships would bring Sutter supplies and ammunition for which he either paid or traded goods. Sutter was quoted as saying, "At times I had more ammo than the whole California government possesses."

One wonders what would have happened if Mexico City had been more understanding of the Russian position and had made a token purchase, allowing Vallejo to administer the facilities? Would the northern California coastal area above San Francisco be more of a metropolitan area today? One also wonders what if the Russians had "called in" their collateral? Taking back Fort Ross and having the facilities at Sutter's Fort would have greatly added to the Russian prestige in California.

The Russians may have had other thoughts about "calling in their paper" due to the large United States naval force off the coast. And don't forget Sutter's 40-brass French cannons—and "all the ammo he ever needed."

—Chapter Eight—

CAPTAIN JOHN AUGUSTUS SUTTER

John Sutter

Captain John Sutter was truly at the right place at the right time when he arrived in California at age thirty-six. He was also very lucky in his early years, and very unlucky in the years following the California gold rush. Sutter has been referred to in many history books as the "Father of American California;" however, there are those that would argue with that designation.

Sutter referred to himself as being Swiss; actually he was born February 15, 1803 in a small German village several miles from the Swiss border. On October 24, 1826, at age twenty-three, he married Annette Dubeld. A day later, the bride presented him with a newborn son whom they named Johann August Sutter, Jr. The proud father was fortunate that his new mother-in-law was quite wealthy, as she backed Sutter financially in several business enterprises, which almost immediately went bankrupt. Sutter had a way for personal extravagances, fancy clothes, lavish food and entertainment. He would grant overly liberal credit to his friends, and incurred recklessly large debts. Facing debtors court, trial, and arrest, Sutter grabbed all the cash he could lay his hands on, kissed his wife and children (by now he had four offspring), and took off for America. As we shall see in the next few pages, things didn't change when he arrived.

When he reached New York, Sutter decided to put more miles between himself and the law, and grabbed a spot on a wagon train heading west. Several German immigrant colonies had sprouted up on the American western frontier near St. Louis and that is where old John was headed. Arriving with empty pockets, he borrowed money from his new found German friends and bought up cheap trinkets, rusty pistols, and old German student jackets from the local pawnshops. In 1835, he joined an expedition to Santa Fe, where he found a ready market for his merchandise. He returned to St. Louis with pockets full of gold. It is unknown if he repaid the loans from his friends; however, while in Santa Fe he had learned all about the golden opportunities that were being offered in California. He decided to pack his saddlebags and find the next wagon train heading west, except that year the wagons were rolling to Oregon, not California.

As Sutter sat around the campfires at night, he found it desirable to invent a fictitious past, so he claimed to his trail-mates that he had gone to military school in France. He had made friends with a fellow student by the name of Louis Napoleon—the future Emperor of France—and had entered the army as a cadet. Sutter conferred on himself the rank of Captain in King Charles' elite Swiss Guard before requesting discharge and heading for America.

Upon arriving at The Dalles, on the Columbia River, Sutter took a few weeks to rest up, then continued his trip by canoe to Fort Vancouver. It was there that John had a burning desire to start a frontier community in California, designed along the lines of the British Fort which was located across the Columbia from Portland, Oregon. His dream was about to materialize, but first he would find himself stuck in Hawaii and Alaska, not by choice, but due to circumstances beyond his control.

Wherever Sutter went, one of the things he was famous for was "hobnobbing" with the rich and influential people in the area. Included were leading merchants, government officials, foreign consuls, and other dignitaries, from whom he would request a letter of introduction.

Sutter was stuck in the Oregon Territory, as no ship was available to go to California. Upon collecting his many introduction letters at Fort Vancouver, Sutter booked passage on a ship sailing for the Sandwich Islands (Hawaii). Upon arriving in Honolulu, he again found no ships leaving for California, so he spent his time becoming acquainted with key people, including King Kamehameha. The King, after hearing of Sutter's military background, urged him to stay and head up the Islands' military. Sutter, of course, turned this offer down, as he really did not have any knowledge of soldiering. While awaiting a ship, he spent his time putting together supplies and enlisting recruits for the California venture. Arranging credit by using his letters of introduction, including

Sutter's Fort today

the one from the King, Sutter was able to buy tools, agricultural implements, weapons, and even two small brass cannons.

The British brig, CLEMENTINE, was set to sail for the Russian settlements in Alaska, and then down to San Francisco to replenish supplies. Sutter approached the ship's captain and arranged free passage for himself, his recruits, and all his supplies. He would act as supercargo for the captain. A supercargo was like a bookkeeper/salesman who handled all trade transactions that were made in each port-of-call. As we have seen in the Fort Ross chapter, the Russian contacts made by Sutter became very profitable to him, particularly the letters of introduction he collected along the way.

—Chapter Nine—

LAND - WATER - SUN

Leo Carrillo was a famous name in modern day twentieth century California, and the family name of Carrillo was predominant throughout the history of Spanish and Mexican California. Leo, among other things, was a very well known and loved actor, movie star, and skilled horseman. January first of each year was a very important date for Leo. The famous Rose Parade in Pasadena, California, was led by Leo, before his death, down the full length of Colorado Boulevard on his magnificent palomino mount, Conquistador, adorned with silver saddle and flowers. Leo wore a bright-colored riding habit.

The first time I saw Leo was at my age of three. My mother and dad would bundle me up against the chilly night air and we would all jump into the old Plymouth about 4:00 AM, leaving West Los Angeles for a two hour drive to Pasadena. This was in the early 1930s before freeways. We would leave early enough in order to not only beat the traffic, but also to gain a spot on the curb of the crowded boulevard. When the parade had started, up near the front would be Leo on his high-stepping horse, Conquistador. Leo was an expert with the *reata* (lasso, in English) and he would twirl it throughout the parade. Spotting this little boy sitting on the curb, he would always come over, lean down from his horse and shake my hand. The crowd loved it and much clapping and cheering would take place. As I grew older and the crowds became larger, my dad would throw a small stepladder in the car because no matter how early we left "West Los," we could never get a place on the curb. I would sit on the top of the ladder in order to see over the crowd. Leo would still wave at me, coming over and standing in his stirrups, he would lean over the crowd to shake my hand. As a young boy I was thrilled at this gesture, but then World War II came along with gas rationing. We never made it back to Pasadena, but I'll always remember that wonderful showmanship put on by my "friend," Leo Carrillo, and his horse, Conquistador.

Leo wrote a book entitled *The California I Love*. I would like to pass on to my readers a couple of stories about the early California Carrillo family members that appeared in the book. These stories involve young señoritas known by the same name: Josefa Carrillo, one from San Diego, the other from Santa Barbara. They were cousins, of course. The "call of the sea" must have had more of a romantic tone for the Carrillo women than what was suspected in the old days. Anyway, both of these stories involve Yankee seafaring captains that fell in love with Carrillo señoritas.

Illustration from Leo Carillo's book, The California I Love, *Prentice-Hall, NJ*

SAN DIEGO JOSEFA

The romance of Josefa from San Diego has come to be known as the most famous elopement in the history of California. To quote our friend Leo Carrillo, "It all happened because a Governor became lovesick like a youth in his teens. He had ants in his pantalones."

The newly appointed Governor of California was known as His Excellency Don Jose Maria Echeandia. According to Leo, the name he bore was almost too heavy for his puny frame to carry. Mexico City appointed Governors to this distant province without being too careful in their selection. When Echeandia took on his new job, he made a short stop in San Diego on his way north to the capital city of Monterey. While attending a fandango given in his honor, he met the most beautiful woman he had ever seen. Her name was Josefa Carrillo.

Travelling on to Monterey after the party, Echeandia found the fog bound town not to his liking. His mind was elsewhere and all he could think about was the beautiful Josefa. "His Excellency" made a decision. He would move the capital of California to San Diego, which didn't make the people of Monterey real happy.

Josefa was the daughter of Don Joaquin and Doña Maria Ignacia Carrillo. The Don and Doña considered it an honor for their daughter to be courted by the governor even though he looked like a shrunken version of a toad. Josefa, when her parents brought up talk of marriage, would say, "I could never have a funny, ugly, little bantam rooster of a man like that!" She would then go on to say, "He makes me want to laugh at him. I'm willing to wait a long time for the man I can truly love. He must be somewhere and I'm not going to marry someone that I could never care for."

`The Don and Doña thought it best to throw a fandango in order to honor the newly appointed Governor and his recent move to San Diego. Perhaps their daughter would warm up to the affection being shown by this most influential newcomer.

An American merchant ship had just arrived from Boston the day before and was now holding "open house" to display all the wares, finery, and latest fashions brought from around the "Horn." The Carrillo's suggested to their daughter that a new dress might be nice for the festive party. Don Joaquin said, "Why not go out to the ship, MARIA ESTA, in the morning and buy the finest silk dress you can find?"

The next day, escorted by her cousin Don Pio Pico, Josefa was rowed out to the ship riding at anchor on the calm waters of San Diego Bay. Many rowboats were plying back and forth to the vessel, carrying all the leading women of the young settlement. Pio Pico helped Josefa up the ship's ladder, then stood by as she looked around in wonder and astonishment at the cargo displayed on the deck. This was her first experience of being a buyer on one of these great ships. Usually it was her mother who did all the buying. Some of the merchandise included shawls from China, pianos and furniture from Boston, serapes from Mexico, and rack after rack of the most beautiful dresses Josefa had ever seen.

Fred Collins cachet #2601

While looking at the dresses, she suddenly felt aware that someone was looking at her. Turning, she looked directly into the light violet eyes of Captain Henry Delano Fitch of New Bedford, Massachusetts. The captain found himself blushing as he stared into the dark luminous eyes of Señorita Josefa. It must have felt like an eternity as they both stared at each other. Finally, cousin Pio Pico came to the rescue, and introduced them to one another.

Speaking fluent Spanish, Captain Fitch asked Josefa if she saw a dress she liked. She responded that she couldn't make up her mind at that moment, but perhaps after resting at the railing for a bit she would again try to make a decision. Actually, her heart was pounding, her mind was in a whirl, all she could think about was this handsome man with the *ojos violados* (violet eyes). Captain Fitch took Josefa up to the bow of the ship and they talked about the beauty of the town spread out before them as well as the countryside and Point Loma. They exchanged their life stories with each other and during that conversation Fitch asked, "Who is that sneaky little fellow on the beach watching us through the spyglass?" Josefa looked closely across the water and said, "That is my suitor, His Excellency, The Governor of California." She then told Fitch about the coming fiesta in the honor of the governor, and asked if Fitch would like to attend. His response was rather brash, as he said, "Are you in love with him? Are you to marry him?" When she said "no" to both questions and added, "I can't stand him," Fitch, with a big smile on his face, said, "I'll most certainly be at the party!"

All of California knew about the governor's courtship, and tongues were wagging from San Diego to Sonoma about this little squirt singing love songs before dawn outside Josefa's window. This serenading in the past had scandalized San Diego but the town was really going to be scandalized by what happened in the next few weeks.

During the days before the fandango was to take place, the young sea captain and Josefa fell more and more in love. She, of course, could not visit the ship each day, but nothing was to stop the captain from coming ashore in a rowboat. Fitch didn't have the ability to sing beneath her window like Echeandia had done, but he still made it plain where his affections lay.

Now came the real problem! Even though an alliance with Governor Echeandia would mean tremendous social and political power for the Carrillo family, the Don and Doña had to admit that Captain Fitch was a very likeable fellow. However, there were other considerations, such as the law and the church, that had to be followed. Captain Fitch was a foreigner, and not a citizen of Mexico, and on top of that, was a non-catholic.

Governor Echeandia made it quite clear to Don Joaquin that these facts made the affair a most serious matter. It was strictly against the law of the land to permit this illegal union to take place between a yankee protestant and the beautiful Josefa.

On the evening of the fiesta, all of San Diego was agog over the preparations, and the air was filled with music and the succulent smell of barbecued meat. It was rumored that Captain Fitch had been given an invitation to the party at the insistence of Josefa, and everyone wondered if he would have the guts to show up. Fitch not only showed up, he was among the first to arrive, and as the music played for the first dance, he presented himself to Josefa and asked her to dance, which she gladly accepted. Throughout the evening Josefa defied her parents and made sport of the governor by dancing time and time again with Fitch. The governor was livid, and glowered at the couple on the dance floor with murder in his eyes. The consensus of the San Diego population was that the governor had lost the contest and that Josefa would never be his.

A few day's after the fiesta Captain Fitch formally asked for the hand of Josefa. The Don and Doña Carrillo diplomatically explained to Fitch that California law forbade such a marriage. Fitch countered the objection by saying he would immediately apply for Mexican citizenship and request baptism as a catholic. The baptism took place the next day at the Chapel of San Diego, where Captain Henry Delano Fitch was given a new name of Enrique Domingo Fitch. The name of Domingo was to honor Domingo Carrillo, uncle of Josefa, who would be the principal witness at the marriage. It was decided that the wedding would take place that next evening. With lots of hustle and bustle it was agreed that it would be a small wedding so as not to embarrass the governor further.

The wedding night arrived with all family members in attendance, including Pio Pico, along with Captain Richard Barry of the Boston clipper ship, VULTURE, acting as best man. The priest was Padre Menendez. The only person missing was Domingo Carrillo, who was to act as witness to the ceremony. Finally, he made his entrance, stating that he was unable to perform the duty as witness. The father of the bride immediately suspected that the governor had threatened Domingo. Echeandia would do anything in his power to have the wedding aborted. Fitch was beside himself and asked Josefa and Pio Pico to step outside where they spoke for over an hour in very soft voices. Fitch then kissed the "bride that wasn't" and stole off into the dark night.

In the morning, before the rays of the sun had replaced the bright moonlight, Pio Pico tapped on Josefa's window. She came forth with a small travelling bag and on horseback the two rode toward the beach. Captain Fitch met them, taking Josefa in his arms and kissed her gently, while shaking hands with Pio Pico. The two lovers then rowed out to Captain Barry's ship, VULTURE, which immediately slipped anchor and silently stole out of the harbor on the morning tide. Soon after, Fitch's ship, MARIA ESTA, also sailed out of San Diego under the command of the first mate, its destination unknown.

When the Carrillo family discovered this scandalous abduction of their daughter they were most upset. San Diego, and indeed all of California, were shaken by the event. It was the most shameful thing that could have happened to a California family. The governor raged and ranted, but there was nothing he could do about the matter. The ships had simply disappeared over the horizon.

A year went by without any word from the young lovers. Then one bright sunny day, a ship named the LEONOR sailed into the bay and dropped anchor. Aboard were Captain Fitch, his wife Josefa, and a tiny infant son. The Carrillo family, still much ashamed by the event, agreed to talk briefly with their daughter and her lover.

In a few days, the Fitch family left San Diego and sailed northward, stopping at San Pedro. Governor Echeandia heard the news and instructed the territorial Vicar and ecclesiastical judge, Padre Sanchez, to arrest Captain Fitch on charges of abduction and other serious counts. Fitch was placed in jail at the San Gabriel Mission. Josefa was not permitted to see or talk to her husband, but was allowed to attend the trial.

All of California was shaken like an earthquake over this scandal. A foreigner had sailed away with one of the most beautiful women of the province in defiance of the law, and the court was going to do something about it. Captain Fitch, representing himself before the court, pleaded eloquently in his defense. He produced evidence of a marriage certificate obtained in Valparaiso, Chile, and the written statement by Curate Orrego that he had performed the ceremony. A statement by Captain Barry of the VULTURE, as witness, was also placed in evidence. The court took over a month to make a decision. Padre Sanchez finally released Captain Fitch.

Upon returning to San Diego, Don Enrique Domingo Fitch and his wife Josefa asked to see her father and mother in private. Pio Pico had sworn them to secrecy, and now they asked the parents to keep secret what they were about to tell.

On the fateful night of the aborted wedding, Pio Pico had arranged with the courageous priest, Padre Menendez, to risk his ecclesiastical standing by returning to the hacienda for a secret midnight wedding ritual. Captain Barry and Pio Pico acted as witness and were sworn to secrecy. This news gave great relief to the Carrillo family, knowing that their daughter sailed to Chile aboard the VULTURE, not as a señorita, but as Señora Fitch. Both parents on hearing this news welcomed the young Fitch family, including the new grandson, with open arms.

SANTA BARBARA JOSEFA

This story, while not as elaborate as the San Diego elopement of Captain Fitch, is quite ironic due to the involvement by the same little amorous Governor Echeandia, as well as a famous sailing ship master by the name of Captain William Dana.

Captain Dana had arrived in Santa Barbara in 1825 and almost immediately fell in love with Josefa upon meeting her at the new commercial store he had just opened. Now don't get Captain Dana confused with Richard Henry Dana who wrote the nautical masterpiece, "Two Years Before The Mast," which was published in 1840. They both came from the same Boston seafaring family and both were well known throughout early California.

Josefa Carrillo was one of five daughters of the prominent Santa Barbaran, Don Carlos Antonio Carrillo. She, like her cousin Josefa of San Diego, also fell madly in love at the first sight of her future husband. It should also be noted that all four of her sisters fell in love and married, Americanos.

Before the romance had blossomed publicly, the leading citizens of Santa Barbara decided they should throw a fiesta in honor of Captain Dana because he had done so much for the town with his trading vessels.

The day of the festivities dawned with much activity of cooking and preparation of delicacies, guitars and violins were being tuned, and all the señoritas and dueñas put on their finest clothing. At last everything was ready, and Captain Dana was escorted to the seat of honor, amid the singing, clapping, and shouts of the fiesta participants. Sitting next to the captain was a young teenage boy who did not speak English; however, this wasn't a problem as Dana spoke fluent Spanish. The boy introduced himself as Pedro Carrillo, younger brother of Josefa. Captain Dana was quite impressed with the youngster's intelligence, self-confident bearing, and command of the language.

The next day Dana approached the parents, Don Carlos Antonio and his wife, and suggested that their son had a bright future when the gates of commerce opened soon in California. Dana recommended that their son accompany him to Boston, where a great Catholic college was available. Pedro could perfect his knowledge of the English language, study law, and become an attorney. It was a tremendous decision to make, but after several days, the Carrillo family agreed that this would be a real opportunity for young Pedro. He would accompany Captain Dana around the Horn on the same ship in which Richard Henry Dana was writing his manuscript.

On the morning Pedro left, his mother walked him to the hacienda gate and said in Spanish, "My boy you are now leaving to study in the great colleges of Boston. You will return a graduate lawyer. What pride reigns in your mother's heart!"

Young Pedro first went to parochial, then preparatory, then law school and graduated. He was away twelve years, all the while his family longing for their educated son to return.

Finally the day arrived, and with church bells ringing from the mission, the whole town ran to the waterfront as the great ship carrying Pedro C. Carrillo, Attorney At Law, was sighted entering Santa Barbara Harbor. Pedro's mother stood by the gate where she had said goodbye to her son so many years before.

As Pedro approached the hacienda gate, his mother could see a change in him. This splendidly dressed young man with his fine mustachio and air of authority was not like the little boy she had kissed goodbye twelve years before. Throwing her arms around Pedro, his mother said in Spanish, "Ah, my son, once more you have returned to the arms of your mother! Now you are a graduate attorney from the great colleges of Boston. What pride reigns in your mother's heart."

Pedro, replying in English with a thick Boston accent said, "Motha, I've been in Bawston so long I cawn't understand a word you say." Señora Carrillo said in English, "The devil you can't," as she picked up a rawhide quirt and gave her son such a licking on the seat of his fancy Boston pants that he forgot all his Boston airs and begged her pardon with great humbleness. The rawhide had cured him of his superiority and New England accent, and we are told that he never ate Boston baked beans again—just California frijoles!

Let us now go back a few years to talk about Josefa of Santa Barbara. While Pedro was learning to speak like a New Englander, his future brother-in-law, Captain Dana, had his hands full with the villain Echeandia. There is no evidence that the Governor wished to marry this other Josefa, but he did cause roadblocks to any wedding between the two lovers. In fact, it took three years before Josefa and William were able to tie the marriage knot.

Fred Collins cachet #2801

Captain Dana was neither a catholic nor Mexican citizen, which made it nearly impossible for him to marry a California girl, or to obtain a land grant. It would be necessary for him to be baptized and naturalized, which old Echeandia blocked repeatedly. One of the problems was the age of the bride. Josefa was only thirteen when she met and fell in love with the sailor. Even after Dana became a catholic and citizen, they had to wait for the bride to become sixteen according to Mexican law.

After the marriage Don Carlos arranged for the couple to obtain the land grant for Rancho Nipomo near San Luis Obispo in 1837, where they lived happily ever after. Besides having twenty-one children, Dana's achievements included service as an appraiser, captain of the port, alcalde of Santa Barbara, and county treasurer after statehood.

As far as Governor Echeandia is concerned, history books are rather unclear as to whether he ever got married, his whereabouts after leaving California are a mystery.

—Chapter Ten—

THOMAS LARKIN

Thomas Oliver Larkin was born in Charlestown, Massachusetts, in 1802 and orphaned at age fifteen. His half-brother was John Rogers Cooper who had arrived in California as captain of a trading schooner in 1823. Cooper married the sister of General Mariano Vallejo and became one of the earliest American settlers in the territory. He later became one of the wealthiest and most successful men in California through his trading activities and land ownership. Because of his excellent family and business connections in this sparsely populated territory, Cooper asked his brother, Thomas Larkin, to join him to help develop business opportunities.

Larkin was well connected in the government, and before he packed his bags and headed for California he was deputized as a "confidential agent," i.e. a master spy, for the United States. Later, in 1842, President John Tyler appointed him American Consul in Monterey thereby legalizing his status as a U.S. government agent and spy.

Thomas O. Larkin

During the trip by sail around the Horn, Larkin met and fell in love with Rachel Hobson Holmes, a widow on her way to Hawaii (Sandwich Islands). They were married and she accompanied him to California.

Foreigners in the early days of Mexican rule could only stay in country by becoming Mexican citizens, marrying into a Spanish family, accepting the Catholic faith, and speaking the language. Larkin had defied this rule by marrying Rachel Holmes. However, he did speak Spanish fluently, and they attended church regularly at the local mission, but he and Rachel never became citizens. The small populace residing in Monterey liked old Tom and his new wife and respected the fact that Cooper was his half-brother, so the law was overlooked. Rachel became the first American woman to live in California, and their children were the first born to American parents. Tom went on to become a super merchant and landowner as he progressed with his assignment.

The United States was interested in the peaceful separation of California from Mexico but realized that this breakaway could only be done once the number of anglo settlers had increased sufficiently. Larkin's orders were to instill this idea into the minds of the native Californios, and to promise them that the United States would support any resistance against Mexican rule. His orders further specified that he should also persuade the locals to resist any overtures made by Britain, France, and Russia towards the acquisition of the territory. In other words, "bring about peaceful American conquest through infiltration and subversion."

John C. Frémont

The entire coastal area of California from San Francisco (actually Sonoma) southward to San Diego consisted of Spanish and Mexican land grants. The Central Valley, because of the Indian menace, had not been utilized for grants by either the Spanish or Mexican governments. Those *ranchos* (large acreage land grants) that were held in the Central Valley were usually held by anglo-saxon or other Europeans that had qualified as naturalized citizens. Christianized Indians held a few of these land grants because under Mexican law they were citizens and entitled to land privileges.

Larkin was involved in the Fremont land deal, paying the sum of $3,000 to purchase *Rancho Las Mariposas* in Fremont's name. Where did Fremont, a warrior and pathfinder, come up with the cash? Gold had not yet been discovered in California—or had it?

Rancho Las Mariposas, a ten-square-league ranch in what is now Mariposa County, was given to Juan Bautista Alvarado in 1844 by Mexican Governor Micheltorena. Thomas Larkin had testified that he had bought Rancho Las Mariposas from Alvarado for $3,000 prior to the Mexican War. Under American law, the granting of land during time of war is not considered valid by the land commission. In the question of Rancho Las Mariposas, this caused a real problem for John C. Fremont and title was litigated for many years before being resolved in his favor in 1856.

During the Bear Flag Revolt, General Vallejo and others had been taken prisoner and held at Sutter's Fort in a spare storeroom. Several heavy bags of freshly minted American gold coins had to be moved to another secure area. It is not likely that Fremont hauled freshly minted gold coins across the mountains in order to pay his troops at the end of the trail. It is more likely to have been American government gold that had come by way of sailing ship and then smuggled ashore under the watchful eyes of Larkin. It appears that Larkin was the keeper of this gold, and that the American government had given him "carte blanche" for any needed expenditures-one of which was the gift of land to fulfill the promise to Fremont upon his return to California from Oregon. Fremont was probably disappointed that Larkin had purchased land along the foothills of the Sierra Nevada instead of along the seacoast. Larkin probably responded that, "someday you'll be grateful for my decision." Remember, this was in the year 1846—long before gold was discovered—or did Larkin know something that others did not?

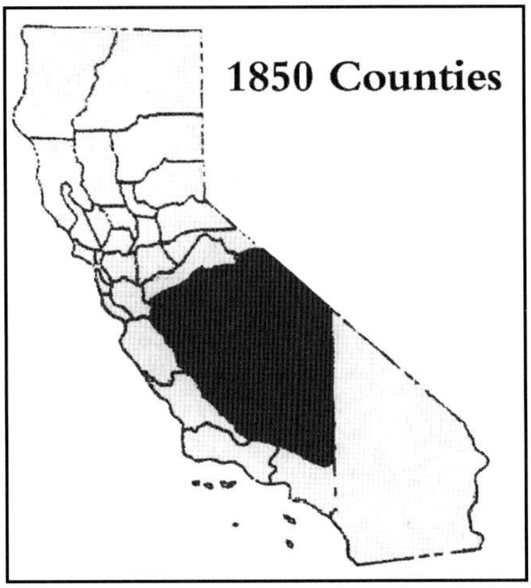

Rancho Las Mariposas, now Mariposa County.

At the conclusion of the war with Mexico the rush for gold in the "Mother Lode" began. Colonel John C. Fremont enlisted a party of Mexican miners from Sonora, and set out to see if any "color" was to be had on the Las Mariposas Rancho. The Colonel didn't have high hopes because the rancho was quite distant from the American and Feather River discoveries to the north. To his great surprise, the creek beds were full of gold, so much, in fact, that the Mexican miners were able to pick up flakes just by dipping a cup in the water. Using knives, they were able to dig gold from the crevices in the bedrock.

This discovery made Fremont a millionaire overnight, yet he was about to begin his journey on the long road to bankruptcy.

First, a flood of miners came south from the Mother Lode. Following closely on their heels were land title experts and attorneys. The miners depleted the rivers and streams of "all that glitters," while the attorneys bled Fremont with legal fees. Fremont could do nothing to stop this rape of his fortune until he had clear title to the Las Mariposas land grant. It was not until 1856 that the U.S. Supreme Court awarded clear title, with all mineral rights, to Fremont.

The main legal problem was the fact that Thomas O. Larkin had purchased the land from Juan B. Alvarado for $3,000 at the time the Mexican War was declared. The original grant was made to Alvarado by Mexican Governor Micheltorena only one year before war was declared. Although perfectly legal, it was the timing of the transaction that was in question. Larkin had put the title in Fremont's name, further complicating the issue.

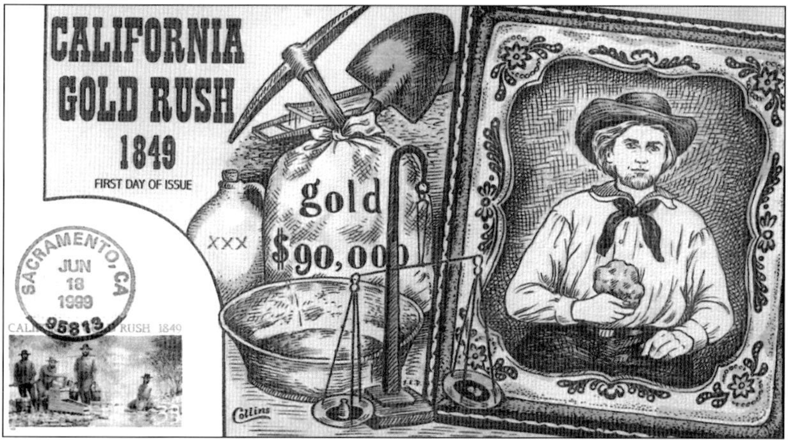

First Day Cover, cachet #W3002, by Fred Collins

The other primary legal problem was that all mineral rights of a land grant were owned by and vested to the Spanish Crown. This mineral ownership passed to the Mexican government when Spain lost the revolution of 1821. Upon the grant to Alvarado, and ultimate sale to Larkin/Fremont, the Mexican government was still vested in the mineral ownership. The land belonged to Fremont, but Mexico owned the gold. With the loss of the war by Mexico, and American takeover of the region, the vested mineral ownership passed to the United States government; however, under American law, when clear land title was awarded, all mineral rights passed to the individual owner.

From 1849 to 1856, Fremont's mineral rights were in question. Trespassers and squatters roamed his ore-rich Mariposa land at will, and upon the court's final decision, Fremont brought in armed men to enforce his rights. Bloodshed and riots broke out as the miners attempted to defend their diggings from being seized and being evicted from their claims.

The miners cannot really be blamed for their ignorance of the law. Most of the land grants in California had been made along the seacoast, and very few along the foothills of the Sierra Nevada. The gold rush bonanza that took place near Sacramento was on public land, not titled land like the Mariposa Rancho. The miners were accustomed to filing a claim for their mines, and then working their claim. When Fremont showed up with guns blazing, the miners were dumfounded and went to war to defend what they thought was legally their claim.

As is proven in the chapter titled, *Pre-Marshall Gold*, "color" was not found on one sunny winter morning in 1848. Many of California's population, including Larkin, knew about the gold, but nothing could be done about it because under Mexican law, all mineral rights belonged to the state. In fact, if there had been a strong Mexican army presence in California anyone found in possession of gold could have been arrested, jailed, or even executed. The Mexican government owned all gold, and it was only upon the American take-over of the territory that the possession of gold became legal.

Larkin's $3,000 investment to lure Fremont and his army of Pathfinders back to California from Oregon was money well spent. If Lt. Archibald Gillespie, U.S.M.C. had failed to make contact with Fremont at Klamath Falls, Oregon, would California history have taken an entirely different course?

—Chapter Eleven—

FORT CATESBY

Most Californians have heard of Fort Tejon, Sutter's Fort, Fort Ross, Fort Bragg, but where is Fort Catesby? Has anybody ever heard of it? Was it a Spanish fort?... a Mexican fort?...an American fort? It has only been about 160 years ago that Fort Catesby played a very important part in the development of our California heritage. It was also our so-called embarrassment. The fort was named after Commodore Thomas Catesby Jones. Let us find out a little more about this unusual affair.

In 1822, California became Mexican territory—a Mexican Department—the result of Spain losing the real estate after the Mexican Revolution in 1821. Nineteen years later it was not Spain that invaded California, it was 150 American Marines and sailors that swarmed ashore at Monterey Bay to replace the Mexican flag with the flag of the United States. Why did this happen? America was not then at war with Mexico; that war didn't start until four years later, in 1846. Did this invasion alert the Mexican government that America had its eye on their territory? Did this incident lead to broken negotiations with Mexico after America offered to buy California? Did it give the British a false signal that led to their build-up of their naval forces in the Pacific? Or was this a message that Thomas Larkin, American consul, wanted to send to the Californios, a group that desired California independence, that America stood behind them in their desire to have a "Texas type" independence from Mexico. Who was Commodore Jones and what were the events that occurred?

Actually, the U.S. Marines and sailors didn't storm the beach, nor was a shot ever fired in anger. But the fact remains that the United States did invade a foreign territory, requested the Mexicans to lower their flag, and replaced it with the stars and stripes. All this occurred four years before the two sides ever got angry enough to declare war!

Commodore Thomas Jones was in charge of the American Pacific Squadron and was the person that was blamed for the foreign policy fiasco. In fact, it has been referred to in most history books as "The Jones Affair." The American Pacific Squadron cruised between Peru to the south, and San Francisco Bay to the north. Their orders were to keep an eye peeled for any military activity by the British or French naval forces, both of which were making overtures of expansion in the area.

Commodore Jones, while on the southern leg of the patrol, had received a copy of a Boston newspaper that stated the Mexicans had sold California to Great Britain for seven million dollars. The paper, of course, was dated several months prior to Jones reading the article. And, as he learned later, the article was written with a little bit of journalistic license.

The American consul in Mazatlan, Mexico, had sent Jones a secret dispatch warning that war between Mexico and America was imminent. When Jones learned that the British Pacific Squadron that had been anchored across the bay from the American fleet in Callao, Peru, had sailed during the night, he interpreted this as a possible move by the British to invade California. The American ships immediately raised their anchors and set sail. As the commodore charged northward, he passed the British fleet near Acapulco, where they had put in to take on supplies. The British really had no intention to invade California; however, Jones continued his mad dash towards Monterey which was the capital of Mexican California.

The California governor was on a trip to Los Angeles, so the *Alcalde* (the equivalent of mayor) of Monterey was requested to come aboard after a meeting between Jones and the American consul in Monterey, Thomas Larkin. Larkin explained to the Alcalde that the British were coming and that it would be necessary to lower the Mexican flag and put the territory under American control.

Larkin had promised the Californios the full support of the United States government if they would consider "Texas Type" independence. The locals, however, were uncertain about this promise made by the American Consul who was 18,000 miles away from Washington by sea. Larkin saw this news about the British as his chance to "walk softly, but carry a big stick" (words made famous by Teddy Roosevelt fifty-some years later). Larkin convinced Jones that the best way to handle the situation was to raise the American flag which the British would honor (not wanting to start a war over California). Larkin then convinced the Alcalde and they both returned to the beach with the 150 sailors and Marines.

With the men at attention the drums rolled, the bugles sounded, the Mexican flag was lowered, and American flag raised to flutter in a strong breeze from the bay. Commodore Jones read a proclamation, then declared that henceforth the presidio would be known as Fort Catesby. A large sign had been made by the ship's carpenter and was hung over the entrance to the drill field.

The next day it was realized that a mistake had been made and that an apology was due the Mexican governor. The Mexican flag was again raised over Monterey. Commodore Jones then sailed south and met the governor in Los Angeles where the formal apology was made on behalf of the United States. It has been said that this "Jones affair" was a great cost, diplomatically, to America; however, the Californios now had their proof that the United States would stand behind them.

Illustration courtesy of the California State Library

The next time you want to win a bet from somebody, use the, "Where is Fort Catesby?" question. I doubt if many Californians know the true location.

—Chapter Twelve—

LIEUTENANT ARCHIBALD GILLESPIE

In November 1845, First Lieutenant Archibald Hamilton Gillespie, U.S.M.C., was ushered into the heavily guarded office. Shaking hands, he said, "Mr. President," and turning to the other gentleman, said, "Mr. Secretary." The door was then closed for the next several hours with no one either entering or leaving. It isn't exactly known what transpired behind that closed door, however, the young Marine officer did receive orders that involved the next several years, which included his reporting back directly, both to the President of the United States, James K. Polk, and the Secretary of the Navy, George Bancroft. In fact, First Lieutenant Archibald Gillespie was more than just a young Marine officer—he was now a full fledged secret agent for President Polk and the United States of America.

In the American conquest for California, Gillespie played an important roll as special messenger from the President of the United States to army pathfinder, John Fremont. Gillespie was a true hero of the campaign and one of the key figures in getting the job done; yet there are no streets, towns, high schools, or even a statue dedicated in his name. He became Captain and Brevet Major of the California Battalion of Mounted Riflemen, and Commandant of the Southern Department of the California Territory during the conquest.

In essence, Gillespie had been ordered to travel through a foreign country—Mexico—wearing civilian attire. Being a military man, he was subject, if caught, to being stood up against a stone wall and shot as a spy. But young Archie had a number of key points to his credit. Not only strongly built and militarily disciplined, he could speak Spanish fluently, had a photographic memory, as well as having great literary skills. All this added to qualities of initiative, courage, and perseverance made him an ideal spy.

Travelling by merchant ship as a civilian, to Vera Cruz, Mexico, in January 1846, Archie learned, upon arrival, that General Paredes had led a revolution taking over the Herrera government in Mexico City. Disguised as an invalid businessman from Cuba, Archie immediately left for Mexico City where he spent a month observing and reporting to the

American consul. Two of his conclusions did more for California independence than any other single item.

Gillespie learned that 400 Mexican troops were to leave Acapulco to strengthen the garrisons in California; however, the troops were diverted at the last moment to Mexico City. Gillespie also reported his opinion of Mexican troop training: "The Mexican Army is ill-fed, poorly equipped, and not an effective fighting force. They are the most miserable troops I have ever seen. The lower ranks are made up of Indian soldiers, and it is a well-known fact that an Indian will follow his officers to the death, but not in this case. The officers were just as bad as the troops." These reports were relayed to Washington, and as we will learn later, American Army General Stephen Kearny, was made aware of Gillespie's opinion of Mexican troops, and it almost cost the general his life at the Battle of San Pasqual.

First Lieutenant Archibald Gillespie would become one of the key figures in the California independence movement. In 1832 he was a sergeant of Marines. In 1833, after being recognized as good officer material by his superiors, he was promoted to second lieutenant, making first lieutenant in 1836. Just prior to the meeting with the President, Lieutenant Gillespie had returned from a two-year cruise aboard the U.S.S. BRANDYWINE that had sailed throughout the Pacific and Indian Oceans, calling at many ports in the Orient. Before landing in Mexico, Lieutenant Gillespie had destroyed all documents and orders, committing these to memory. It was fortunate he did so, as the Mexican Army searched his luggage in every town from Mexico City to Mazatlan. The one mistake he made was when he referred to himself as a merchant from Cuba, he also stated he was travelling to China. Upon arriving in Mazatlan, his first visit was with Commodore John D. Sloat, Commander of the United States Pacific Fleet. Commodore Sloat pointed out that if Gillespie were planning to arrange transportation to California and not embark on a ship heading for China, the Mexicans would realize he was a spy. It would be less obvious if he bummed a ride on the Sloop-Of-War, U.S.S. CAYNE, which was leaving for the Sandwich Islands (Hawaii) the next day. Sloat would then give the ship's captain orders to do a turn around and sail from the Sandwich Islands to Monterey, California, where Gillespie was to call on the American consul, Thomas Larkin, with the orders from President Polk.

Upon the arrival of the U.S.S. CAYNE at Monterey, the Mexicans became suspicious of this civilian that had disembarked from a United States naval vessel. Soldiers were assigned to shadow his every move. Basically, Polk's orders to Larkin, as well as Fremont, who had just departed Monterey for Sacramento, was for a peaceful annexation of California to the United States. It would be the job of Larkin and Fremont to stir up the Californios against Mexican rule and declare independence similar to the Texas Revolution in 1836, but without bloodshed.

Gillespie, upon learning that Fremont had left, borrowed several horses from Larkin and gave chase. Upon his arrival at Fort Sutter, Gillespie was again disappointed to learn that Fremont and his band of explorers had just left for Oregon. John Sutter knew something was in the wind when Gillespie presented himself as a representative of President Polk. John Sutter recognized Gillespie's name from a roster of officers when the U.S.S. BRANDYWINE had called at Monterey several years earlier upon returning from the Orient.

Gillespie immediately took off after Fremont and his party, as these people were the key to the United States takeover of California. Fremont had just entered Oregon, near Klamath Falls, when the "moccasin telegraph" caught up to him with the news that a U.S.M.C. officer was desperately trying to reach him. Fremont reversed his trail and arrived at Gillespie's camp just in the nick of time to help fight off an Indian raid that would have wiped out the messenger from Washington.

Fremont and Gillespie then immediately returned to Sutter's Fort. One of the orders from President Polk was the abolishment of Fremont's title as explorer and the reversion back to being an officer in the United States Army. On the one hand, this would mean the wearing of his uniform to instill faith among the Californians that the United States had an interest in the territory. On the other hand, Fremont was not to act in any capacity of a government employee when selling the idea of a peaceful revolution by the Californians against Mexico City.

Contrary to the verbal orders Gillespie had given Larkin, it was Fremont's understanding that, if possible, he was to goad the Mexican Army into attacking the American settlers. This would allow the United States to send military forces to California in order to protect American lives and property. The Bear Flag Revolt is a prime example of Fremont wearing two hats in his diplomatic approach to the problems. Gillespie also relayed to Fremont that war with Mexico was imminent and that the Army of the West was being formed at that very moment to march on California and bring relief to Fremont's small band of men. In addition, as a reward for Fremont's loyalty and support, a land deal was being put together by Larkin, whereby Fremont would become one of the wealthiest Americans in the territory to help augment any future political aspirations he may have.

—Chapter Thirteen—

MOUNTAIN DOLPHINS

This chapter title may sound a little fishy, but it is not! It's about John Charles Fremont and his lost mountain howitzer. Fremont had not really lost his cannon, he just abandoned it during his second expedition to Oregon and California. The whereabouts of the cannon remains a mystery even today. Is it still in a canyon somewhere in the High Sierras, covered by brush and snow? Did the Indians find the cannon and bury it a few hundred yards away from where Fremont left it? Some claim that the cannon sitting in the museum at Carson City, Nevada, is the one Fremont hauled all over the countryside. Others claim that the gun in Carson City is the one captured by the Californios at the battle of San Pasqual. An examination of the evidence is in order.

First, it is important to know the difference between a mountain howitzer and a field howitzer. It is also necessary to understand the difference between a gun and a howitzer—both are referred to as cannons. The development of mountain artillery began in France in 1821 after the Napoleonic Wars proved that field pieces were often too cumbersome for use in mountainous regions. The Spanish had used small mountain howitzers, which proved superior in mobility and usefulness against the French field guns, which only shot a projectile on a flat trajectory. The howitzer on the other hand could fire a round in a much higher and arcing flight. The French guns required a higher elevation, or a clear field of fire, so that friendly soldiers were not endangered. Conventional artillery due to its weight, wide wheel-base, and gun-barrel elevation limitations, proved to be unsuited for narrow footpaths and steep slopes.

The painting reproduced in this chapter showing Mongol troops under Genghis Khan attacking the Chinese in a battle from the 1200s is a perfect example of an elevated mountain cannon. The Chinese had invented this small cannon many centuries before the French and Spanish came up with the idea.

An example of a gun firing a projectile on a flat trajectory would be those used on old sailing ships. The gunner would use the roll of the ship to plan his elevation depending on whether his target was the rigging or waterline of the enemy ship being fired upon.

Chinese mountain cannon. Illustration from the Gallistan Library, Tehran, Iran.

What is the significance of the term, dolphin? The great cannons on sailing ships usually had handles on top of the barrel in order to more easily move the heavy guns from place to place with a block and tackle. Field pieces on land did not require the handles as the gun carriage, with large wheels, were used to reposition the weapon. The handles on the naval cannons would sometimes take on an ornamental design of playful dolphins as they skipped along on the surface of the sea. As we progress through this chapter, you'll find that dolphins on the small mountain howitzer are ornamental only, and have no function other than for identification.

John Charles Fremont was proficient in botany, geology, astronomy, and navigation. He was also an excellent map maker and sketch artist—but he was not a military tactician. His career started with the United States Navy as a mathematics teacher aboard the Sloop-of-War, U.S.S. NATCHEZ, which was used as a training ship for midshipmen since the United States Naval Academy had yet to be established. After a two-year world cruise, Fremont was appointed as Professor of Mathematics in the navy, but he turned down the position and instead applied for a commission with the United States Topographical Corps in 1837, then a unit of the U.S. Army. Soon after Fremont's commission as a lieutenant in the army came through, he met and fell in love with Jesse Benton, the fifteen-year-old daughter of Senator Thomas Hart Benton and Elizabeth Benton. The senator was one of the most powerful and influential men in American politics. The senator's wife, Elizabeth, wanted her daughter to marry President Martin Van Buren, who had expressed an interest in Jesse. Fremont had no money, no family, and his prospects for army promotion would be slow, but he continued a daily courtship of Jesse as their love for each other grew. Senator and Mrs. Benton desperately needed to split the couple up, so arrangements were made to send Fremont on a map making expedition to the Rocky Mountains.

On June 4, 1841, Fremont mounted up and led an expedition through the gates at Fort Leavenworth, Kansas. Four months later he returned to Jesse whose love had only grown stronger. On October 19, 1841 they were married in a secret ceremony and then finally accepted into the Benton family. It turned out to be a great love affair that lasted until Fremont's death on July 13, 1890.

During Fremont's life his achievements were many. He was the first senator from the newly admitted state of California. In 1856 he was the first presidential candidate from the newly formed Republican Party. During the Civil War, he was a Major General in the Union Army. He was appointed Governor of the Arizona Territory from 1878-1881. Fremont also went through some rough times beginning with his court martial at the end of the Mexican War by General Kearny for disobeying orders. He went bankrupt trying to prove ownership and legal title to the largest gold bearing land grant in California history.

But what was the story of the lost cannon that was hauled all over the west behind a mule?

During the first half of the 1800's most United States Army and Navy heavy guns were purchased or received as gifts from other nations or they were captured in battle. In June 1836, the United States Army ordered a dozen bronze mountain howitzers from Cyrus Alger & Company of South Boston, Massachusetts. The tubes were delivered in 1837. The carriages and caissons ordered from the Watervliet Arsenal of West Troy, New York, were delivered at the same time. Bronze is an alloy of tin and copper, and those tubes coming from Cyrus Alger contained 90% copper and 10% tin. Brass is an alloy of zinc and copper.

In 1847, Lt. Col. George Talcott, Assistant to Commander of the United States Army Ordnance Department, wrote a history of American cannons titled, "The Talcott Bronze System of Ordnance," in which he makes the statement, "Brass is not acceptable because of high cost."

The early French cannons could not be disassembled, while most

Spanish howitzers were able to be disassembled. Ammunition, carriage, wheels, and tube were carried on the backs of several mules, and the howitzer was hastily reassembled at time of battle. There is no evidence that Fremont, while covering over 1,300 miles of trail, ever disassembled his howitzer. If he could have, it is likely that he would have saved the barrel rather than abandoning it because of its inherent value. Fremont most likely had a howitzer of French manufacturer, as the American-made bronze cannons delivered to the United States Army in 1837 all were able to be disassembled. In addition, none of the American-made Cyrus Alger howitzers had any ornamental handles on top.

It is interesting to note that what are referred to as Russian guns, are actually French, that had been captured in the war with Napoleon.

Now comes the mystery! During the California portion of the Mexican War, there were known to be at least six mountain howitzers in the region. Two brass cannons, of unknown origin, had been brought to California from Hawaii by John Sutter. Two bronze, United States Army cannons, had been with the Kearny expedition, one of which had been captured by the Californios at San Pasqual. Another cannon had been brought to San Pasqual by Marine officer, Archibald Gillespie. This cannon is believed to have been one owned by Sutter and captured by the Californios near Los Angeles and then recaptured by United States forces. The sixth gun would have been Fremont's. There may have been more of the little cannons since Russia had sold forty guns from Fort Ross to Sutter, however, most of those had been field pieces.

The Russian (French?) guns had dolphin handles as evidenced by the Naval cannon image on page 68. It has been documented that two howitzers, whether made in France or Russia, had been given to Sutter. One of these was lost in the 1906 San Francisco earthquake, the other is on display at Fort Ross. Please note the ornamental handles on top of the tube.

When Fremont was preparing for his second expedition west he submitted a request to the St. Louis Armory for a mountain howitzer. Col. Stephen Kearny had to approve all requests of this nature, and had taken a personal dislike to Fremont. Kearny believed that there was no way a scientific mission would require artillery. Fremont argued that the weapon was needed to protect against aggressive Indian attacks. Not wanting to give up a brand new bronze United States Army model 1837 howitzer, Kearny allowed Fremont to take one of the brass models which was actually of French manufacture and given to the army as a gift from the French government. Kearny made no mention that the howitzer couldn't be disassembled, but did point out that the handles would come in handy for transporting the weapon.

The mountain howitzer sitting in the Carson City museum is known and referred to as the "Fremont Cannon," and this is most likely a true statement—however, it is not Fremont's "lost cannon."

Naval Cannon, note the handles that were often fashioned as dolphins. Illustration courtesy of the California State Library.

When the Army of the West, led by General Stephen Kearny, (he had been promoted from Colonel to General upon his victory at Santa Fe) came down from the hills to engage the Californios at San Pasqual, it brought two bronze model 1837 mountain howitzers. During the conflict, one howitzer was lassoed by a Mexican lancer and dragged away from the field of battle. The howitzer was returned, but not until the surrender by Andros Pico near Los Angeles and then the howitzer was returned to Fremont—not Kearney! This irritated General Kearny to no end and was part of his reason to court martial Fremont and bring disgrace upon him.

Fremont finally agreed to take the howitzer to Monterey for a victory parade and then to San Francisco for display. The howitzer was subsequently taken across the mountains to Carson City and to this day is pointed out to tourists as, "Fremont's Gun." But the truth is, it is the Fremont/Kearny gun with 1837 stamped on the tube. It can be disassembled and there are no dolphin handles to be seen.

Is additional proof needed? The topographer and cartographer on several Fremont expeditions was a man named George Carl Ludwig Preuss. Preuss was an expert, and the best in the west at drawing very accurate pictures of all hills, lakes, outcroppings, and even small rocks

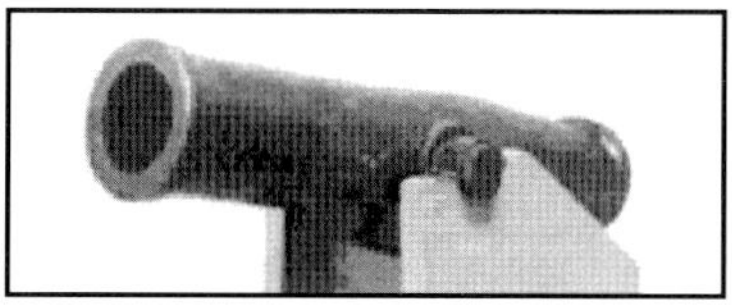

"Fremont's Cannon," Carson City, Nevada museum

along the trail. Remember, this was before photography and cameras, and artists and illustrators were used to record visual aspects of exploratory expeditions.

Several days had been spent at Pyramid Lake resting both men and animals before tackling the High Sierras from the east, or Nevada side, of the mountains. With drawing instruments in hand, Preuss began his sketch of the California camp. Included in the drawing was the little mountain howitzer, clearly showing the dolphin handles on top. His drawing is presumed to be accurate, since it is unlikely that he had ever seen other cannon with ornamental dolphin handles.

Preuss disliked the cannon as can be seen from his journal entry on December 1, 1843. "Here I am in the mountains, sitting on an old fir trunk, with the snow around me and a mule beside me, waiting the caravan. I had to give up my place in the wagon. Fremont said that progress was too slow on the bad road and gave the wagon away. Yet the cannon causes just as much delay, and unless he presents it to someone as he did the wagon, we shall move ahead slowly." Preuss had earlier written an entry as follows: "At a bad place the gun carriage of the howitzer broke, and it took time to repair it. If we had only left that ridiculous thing at home."

Fremont's mountain howitzer, California State Library

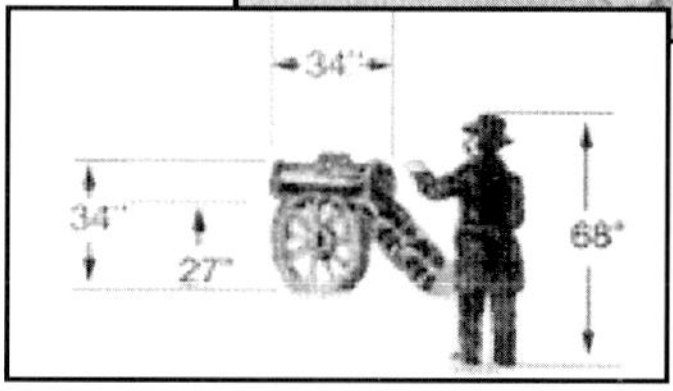

On January 29, 1844, Fremont made the decision to abandon the howitzer. The snow at the 8,000-foot level was very deep; the men and animals were tired and starving; the terrain was savage.

On March 8, 1844, the twenty-six men, more skeletal than human, and their animals stumbled through the gate to Sutter's Fort near Sacramento, California. This second expedition, and its return to St. Louis, would be completed at a later date, but only after the snows had melted that spring.

Somewhere high up in the Sierra Nevada, and possibly deep down in a ravine, lies a little brass howitzer. The carriage and large wheels most likely will have rotted away; however, the brass tube, tarnished by age, would still be intact. The location of this little gun that had bounced along behind Fremont and his group for over 3,900 miles of western trails is within thirty miles of Bridgeport, California. The exact location is said to be in the Pickle Meadows area, high up in the most dangerous, formidable, and forbidding part of the mountain range. It is at so high an altitude that a visitor is left breathless. Pickle Meadows is also a military base. The area is controlled by the United States Marine Corps, and used for cold weather training. Permission to scout the area might be obtained in the summer months, but beware—rattlesnakes control the region in the dry season!

A forty-niner gold-mining slogan is as appropriate for Fremont's howitzer as it is for finding gold: "You never know if you are one foot from a million dollars, or a million feet from one dollar." The little gun today would be priceless. Many seeking this fortune in the past may have only been a few feet away from it while trekking through the thick underbrush.

—Chapter Fourteen—

PRE-MARSHALL GOLD

John Augustus Sutter and his sidekick partner, James W. Marshall, had kept the secret long enough. It was now time to shout the news to the world. The date was January 24, 1848 when Marshall leaned over the railing at the Sutter's Mill, spotted "color" in the water, and yelled, "Eureka." Thus gold was "officially" discovered in California and the legendary gold rush was about to begin. But was this truly the first time that gold had been discovered in the state? An examination of some events which preceded this discovery is in order.

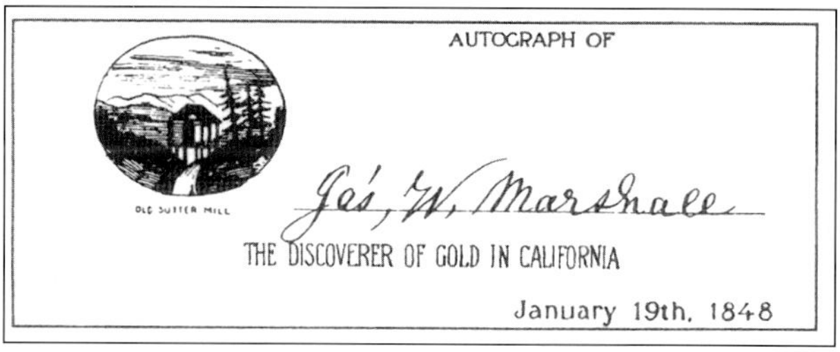

Illustration from Pictorial History of California, *Doubleday, NY*

In the winter of 1846-47, Bill Johnson was one of the Mormons working for Sutter, and he was quoted as saying, "We had been finding gold right along up there at Sutter's. Marshall and Sutter both said it was only mica." Johnson also said that he and his partners would take turns travelling to San Francisco with small amounts of gold, and selling it to ship captains. The captains would pay them $8.00 per ounce and told the Mormons to go back to wherever they found the stuff and bring back as much as possible. These ship captains were pretty shrewd people—they knew gold when they saw it, and they knew it would bring at least $17.00 per ounce in Boston. The price of refined gold at the mint was $19.00 per ounce. Not a bad deal—more than double their money in a few short months!

As an example of the ship captains' shrewdness, they would take otter skins to the Orient, where they received top dollar for the cargo. If the skins were worth $60,000, a deal would be made with the Chinese merchant to give a receipt for $40,000 and slip $10,000 under the table to the captain. Thus the merchant was happy, the captain was happy, and the ship's owners were happy, as the $40,000 was all profit, having only cost a few trinkets for the Indians in trade. The ship captain had his cash from the transaction and could purchase all of the California gold he could lay his hands on. And he didn't have to split the profits with the ship owners. Not a bad deal!

The following items, in chronological order, are further proof that gold was not originally discovered one sunny California morning on January 24, 1848. This information is from the book *Pre-Marshall Gold In California, Volume II* by Emil H. Bunje, Ph.D. and James C. Kean, Historic California Press, 1983.

1839	George C. Yount discovers gold on Catalina Island.
1840	Early 'mission gold' discoveries made public for first time.
1841	Baptiste Ruelle discovers gold in Los Angeles County.
	Interest in gold spreads among American immigrants.
	Thomas Larkin exports 100 ounces of gold to East Coast.
1842	Vein of virgin gold found near San Fernando Mission.
1842	Commercial quantities of gold found at Placerito Canyon by Francisco Lopez.
	Emissary sent to Mexico City with report on Lopez discovery.
	Detailed information on Lopez placers sent to Governor. First authentic shipment of California gold to a U.S. Mint.
1843	Lopez makes second discovery in San Feliciano Canyon.
	Gold found near Santa Ynez Mission in Santa Barbara County.
	Jose Salazar takes out $42,000 in nuggets from San Feliciano.
	Many professional miners from Sonora arrive at Placerito.
	Baptiste Ruelle informs Sutter and Bidwell of gold find on the American River.
1844	Pablo Gutierrez tells Bidwell of gold in the Bear River.
1845	The 'Southern Quarterly' reports rich veins of gold in heart of California.
	Miss Bonney discovers gold not far from Sutter's Fort.
1846	John Fremont hints of gold existence in his report to

Washington.

Consul Larkin reports export of 200 ounces in one shipment.

L.W. Sloat informs New York that California is rich in gold.

1847 Captain Charles Bennett finds gold near Sutter's Fort.

1848 George Evans extracts $19,000 worth of gold from Mormon Island.

Bill Johnson finds gold at Sutter's Mill prior to Marshall.

1848 James Wilson Marshall discovers gold at Coloma January 24.

It is true that the first commercially extracted gold to any degree was found by Marshall; however, did the mountain men, the first settlers, the hunting parties, and others, who came over the Sierras years before know about the presence of gold? Were they all blind? There is other proof of placer gold found prior to the Marshall discovery.

Famous desert rat and prospector, Thomas Long "Pegleg" Smith, left Yuma in 1829 on a trip to Los Angeles by way of the Warner Ranch. Being familiar with the desert, Pegleg decided to leave the old trail and take a short cut; however, he became lost after a sudden and violent storm passed through the area. Pegleg climbed three adjacent hills to take sightings of the route. On top of one hill, a large quantity of heavy black lumps caught his attention. Thinking these were examples of "native copper," he picked up several and placed them in his saddlebags to add to his collection of oddities. Upon reaching Los Angeles, Pegleg showed the lumps to an old mining friend.

The old miner added some acid to the samples and was able to remove the black coating, exposing the brilliant gold color of the nuggets. Taken for assay, it showed 70% gold, 20% silver, and 10% copper. It was the copper that had oxidized and gave the nuggets their black color.

Old pegleg retraced his steps through the desert, but he never found the three hills again. In 1880 a half-breed Indian who lived near the Warner Ranch, went into the desert and after three days he returned with enough gold to satisfy his needs. When the Indian died several years later from a knife wound he received in a bar fight, $4,000 worth of black gold nuggets were found in his cabin.

Two things stand out about Pegleg Smith's discovery. First, it was twenty-one years before the discovery at Sutter's Mill. Secondly, all the gold taken from the Mother Lode country during the gold rush of the 1850s contained 10% to 20% silver alloy, but no copper, with one exception: the gold nuggets from Calaveras County contained 20% silver and 10% copper!

After Spain lost control of their provinces in the New World in 1821, the wealthy Peralta mining family from Sonora, Mexico had a secret mining operation in the Sierra foothills. The Peraltas made no attempt to process the gold in California; instead they shipped the ore by long pack trains to Sonora.

The three Peralta sons were in charge of this secret operation, along with their foreman, Juan Valdez. When the next pack train was to leave, the Peralta boys informed Valdez that they would meet him on the trail about half way to Sonora. The lads had decided to ride into Los Angeles for a few days of merriment.

Juan Valdez moved swiftly down the old Indian trail leading the team of burros and horses through the western foothills of the Sierras. The trail would eventually bring them to the desert crossing area near what is now Barstow, California. Soon the hot winds of the desert would make life miserable for Juan and his animals until he reached the cantinas in Sonora, Mexico. Each burro was laden with many sacks of gold nuggets, all taken from the rich riverbeds of the high Sierra. Juan knew that his personal percentage of the gold's value would buy him many beers at the cantina. *Una más, por favor*!

When the Spanish controlled Northern Mexico and California, the population of the territories was very sparse. Most people lived either in the coastal areas or on large land grants in the valleys and flatlands. The Spanish military presence was also very limited with only small outposts on the frontier. The main army was stationed further south in Mexico City. The Baja, a desolate desert, had more rattlesnakes than humans.

The Spanish explorers knew about the presence of gold almost from the beginning, after all the search for gold (*siete ciudades de oro*) was one of the primary reasons for the exploration of the northern territories. It was kept a secret because the Spanish could not openly mine, process, and transport the gold without causing problems for the owners of the haciendas and ranchos. The Mexican revolution in 1821 freed the people from those constraints and opened the Sierras to Mexican exploration.

The population still remained sparse, the Mexican military was more thinly spread than the Spanish military had been, but it was still in the best interest of the Mexican government to keep the secret about the "gold in them thar hills." As more *Norte Americanos* flooded into the state the government was truly concerned about the influence the "foreigners" would have on Mexican control of the territory. So the gold was still moved down through the foothills and across the desert to Sonora without advertisement or fanfare.

The California gold rush that could have been, in the early 1840s, never came about because the land grants were controlled by old established families. It was the government's gold under Mexican law, and not open to claim as it would be later under United States law. The majority of Californios were already wealthy due to their trade in hides and tallow, and were not seeking additional sources of income. They were comfortable in their way of life and didn't want a lot of people disturbing their lands.

Juan and his helpers had traveled these trails bringing out the gold for many years. Normally, only deer and a few bears were met along the trail, and occasionally an Indian or two. The Indians had no use for gold; their only interest was hunting and fishing. Juan made sure that his burros carried food and a supply of trinkets for the Indians on the return trip from Sonora. But today as Juan crossed the desert he had the misfortune of meeting up with a large Indian hunting party. Without any gifts on this southern trek to Sonora, Juan realized he was in trouble and had better get the burros "in gear and vamoose." After a chase of several miles Juan paid a high price by losing his scalp. The Indians rounded up the horses and burros and drove them many miles off the trail to the top of a high knoll. The cargo was dumped on the ground and the animals driven back to the Indian village. As previously stated, the Indians had no use for white man's gold, but the captured animals would provide many enjoyable hours of roasting steaks around the campfires. The Peralta family would never find this lost caravan of gold, but would continue for years "salting" the mines of Sonora with California gold.

As we have seen in the chronological report, in 1842 and 1843 there was one man named Francisco Lopez that could lay claim against Marshall's title as the discoverer of California gold. Lopez was a well-to-do and very educated rancher living near Mission San Fernando. While herding cattle on March 9, 1842 he stopped to rest under the shade of a large oak tree. His wife had given him orders to bring home some wild onions for their evening meal, and much to his surprise, there were onions between the large roots of the oak. Lopez started to dig the wild onions with his knife, when he noticed shining particles clinging to the roots. Curious, he dug deeper and found gold nuggets. Several days later, Lopez rode into Los Angeles to verify his discovery and it was determined that the glittering pebbles were indeed gold. In the next year, over $100,000 in nuggets and dust came from the Lopez' placers, and was shipped to the United States mint at Philadelphia. During the next twenty years, over 6,000 prospectors swarmed through the Placerito and San Feliciano canyons and mined over $5,000,000 worth of gold. Today the area is designated as a state historic park.

John Sutter

It is somewhat remarkable that for years the secret of gold remained unrevealed in the High Sierras. Trappers, emigrants, explorers, natives, and even professional scientists had reported nothing while trudging the trails.

As proof that Sutter had knowledge that gold existed prior to Marshall's discovery, his own words from his book, *The Discovery of Gold in California*, provide this evidence:

"...Mister Dana of the scientific corps of the expedition under Commodore Wilkes' Exploring Squadron told me that he had the strongest proof and signs of gold in the vicinity of Shasta Mountain, and further south. A short time afterwards, Doctor Sandels, a very scientific traveler, visited me, and explored a part of the country in a great hurry, as time would not permit him to make a longer stay. He told me likewise that he found sure signs of gold, and was very sorry that he could not explore the Sierra Nevada. He did not encourage me to attempt to work and open mines, as it was uncertain how it would pay and would probably be only for the Mexican government. So I thought it more prudent to stick to the plow, not withstanding I did know that the country was rich in gold, and other minerals. An old attached Mexican servant who followed me here from the United States, as soon as he knew that I was here, and who understood a great deal about working in placers, told me he found sure signs of gold in the mountains on Bear Creek, and that we

Fred Collins cachet #W3001

would go right to work after returning from our campaign in 1845, but he became a victim to his patriotism and fell into the hands of the enemy near my encampment, with dispatches for me from Governor Micheltorena, and he was hung as a spy, for which I was very sorry."

It is interesting to note that Spanish law did not allow individuals to own mineral rights. Silver and gold were owned by the Spanish crown and this law was adopted by the Mexican government. "Under Mexican law, no interest in the minerals of gold and silver passed by a land grant from the government, unless expressly so designated." Under American law, the conveyance of full land title includes all minerals and mineral rights.

It would not be a surprise to find that Sutter, Vallejo, Larkin, Fremont, and others knew about the difference in the laws of the two countries and did not push for the "official" discovery of gold until after California became part of the United States, and that they all were in favor of peaceful revolution against Mexican rule.

—Chapter Fifteen—

GENERAL STEPHEN WATTS KEARNY

The only battle lost by the United States in the Mexican War was in California and was fought in San Diego County. It was only a minor skirmish, but it had a strange conclusion: The United States Cavalry who usually ride to the rescue in Hollywood western films, had to be rescued by the United States Marine Corps, along with sailors from the U.S. Navy.

In the war, which lasted from 1846 to 1848, ninety-nine percent of the 1,700 Americans who were killed died outside of California. The other one percent died in California at the Battle of San Pasqual, or two smaller actions that took place near Los Angeles. It could be said that the deaths of this handful of fallen American heros accounted for the addition of all of the land that in later years would become the states of Nevada, Utah, Arizona, New Mexico, parts of Wyoming and Colorado and, of course, all of California.

Why did the United States fight an unpopular war with Mexico? There were many reasons, mostly political, accompanied by some sword rattling by Britain and France, but basically the war was started when Texas declared independence from Mexico on March 2, 1836.

Texas petitioned the United States to be annexed that same year, but was refused primarily because Mexico declared that it would view annexation as an act of war. Nine years later, the leaders in Washington wanted to either buy California from Mexico or go to war to obtain it. Texas was admitted to the Union on March 1, 1845, provoking Mexico to declare war fourteen months later on May 13, 1846.

Meanwhile in California, there were a number of factions at work. The wealthy Mexican landowners and their employees, known as the "Californios," wanted an independence from Mexico similar to that of the Republic of Texas. The newly arriving settlers from the United States, who were being ruled firmly by the Mexican army, wanted to be a state in the union of the United States of America. The Mexican nationals wanted, of course, to continue to be a province of Mexico. The Indians, the true Native Americans, just wanted to be left alone. In this boiling cauldron, something had to give, and the act which precipitated open warfare was Fremont's defiance of the expulsion orders of Mexican Army Comandante General Jose Maria Castro. Fremont and his band of explorers were not about to leave California after receiving the secret orders from Washington relayed by Lieutenant Archibald Gillespie.

The war with Mexico was six weeks old when General Kearny, a veteran and hero of the War of 1812, rode out through the main gate at Fort Leavenworth, Kansas, leading the Army of the West. His mission was to occupy New Mexico, then march on to California. President Polk expected him to reach California before winter set in. Kearny sent a scouting party ahead of his 1,700 man main force with orders to deliver a message to the Governor of the Mexican province who resided in Santa Fe. The message was short and to the point. "We come seeking a union with the United States, and would suggest no resistance from you, or your troops, that you may have available." The Army of the West rode into Santa Fe without a shot being fired, and raised the stars and stripes on August 18, 1846.

It was then that General Kearny made the first of his many mistakes. Because of the easy victory and his expectation of the same in California, he set out with only 300 men, leaving the remainder as occupational troops in Santa Fe. Eleven weeks were to pass before the battered and tattered remnants of his Army limped into San Diego. It became one of the longest and most grueling marches in United States military history.

The next mistake was requiring the troops to ride large military mounts, while mules were used to pull wagons and two howitzers. Navajo and Apache Indian raids were frequent in the New Mexico territory, and Kearny would send his dragoons in pursuit. The more appropriately mounted Indians would easily disappear into the mountains. All this effort was time consuming, and each day brought his army closer to the winter deadline.

Kit Carson had been instructed by Fremont to carry dispatches from

Los Angeles to Washington, advising the President that the war had been all but won in California. Carson, with his party of fifteen Americans and Indian guides, had traveled 1,000 miles in thirty-one days. Reaching the Rio Grande, they turned northward towards Taos, New Mexico, as Carson wanted to visit his wife before striking out across the country to Washington. Halfway up the Rio Grande to Albuquerque, Carson was surprised when he spotted the long column of wagons and the Army of the West coming towards him. Upon advising General Kearny that the United States flag flew over every major town in California, the General requested Carson join his force as a guide across the desert and mountains to the west. Carson refused the request, since he wanted to meet President Polk, as well as visit with Mrs. Carson. General Kearny gained the upper hand when he learned that Fremont had promoted Carson from frontiersman and scout, to a lieutenant in the United States Army. The general then ordered Carson to join the column while his party continued on to Washington without him.

The next mistake by Kearny, when he learned that the American flag flew throughout California was to order two-thirds of the dragoons to return to Santa Fe. By now it was October 9 and the column had only covered 200 miles in two weeks. Carson advised the general that the wagons were worthless in the mountainous terrain they would encounter because it was strewn with rocks and boulders. Also, the crossing of the desert would be a hazard without water or grass for the horses. It was Carson's estimate that it would take four months to reach the coast. This time-table could be cut in half using only mules and packsaddles. Kearny instructed that the wagons and most of the horses be returned to Santa Fe, along with the dragoons. Another week was lost in camp awaiting the mules and packsaddles coming from Santa Fe.

Kearny's Army of the West; illustration courtesy of The Call to California, *Union-Tribune Publishing Co.*

Finally they broke camp and headed west along the Gila River, which flows through the rugged mountains of present-day New Mexico and Arizona. On November 9, the weary column finally departed the Arizona mountains and emerged onto the plain. The animals were completely worn out. The men were instructed to dismount and walk, and because of the lack of water, grass, and food supplies, one-half ration was the order of the day—and they still had the cruel California desert to face—a place that it was said "God had forgotten." It had also been said that "the desert has room for anything, except a mistake."

While taking a day to rest the animals before tackling the desert, a scouting patrol captured a Mexican messenger on his way to Sonora. In searching this *hombre*, dispatches were found that made it clear that an uprising had occurred in Los Angeles and that, "The detestable anglo-yankee yoke had been overthrown, and the Mexican flag once again flew proudly over California." Kearny was stunned at this news. He had given up two-thirds of his tiny army, and the remainder was about to enter enemy territory, undernourished and exhausted, with pack animals that could barely stand up, and mounts that could barely hold the weight of their riders. Over two months on the march had taken a heavy toll on the dragoons, as well as the mules and horses. Many uniforms hung in shreds, cactus tore at their bare legs, boots had been split open, and were worthless even though bound with rags to protect against the hot sand, stones, and cactus.

The morning of December 2 found the Army of the West at the western edge of the desert, and a short uphill ride later it came to the Warner Ranch, which is located east of Palomar Mountain in San Diego County. Kearny found that old man Warner was a prisoner of the Americans in San Diego due to his unsympathetic attitude to the American take-over of California. After resting for a day, the army traveled southward fifteen miles to the Stokes' Santa Ysabel ranch, near the town of Ramona. Here they rested another day, while Stokes volunteered to carry a message to Commodore Stockton in San Diego. Upon receiving the message, Stockton immediately sent off a welcome force of a dozen sailors, along with twenty-six riflemen from the California Battalion, under the command of Lieutenant Archibald Gillespie, U.S.M.C. and Lieutenant Beale of the Navy. This group of Americans traveled east to El Cajon, then headed northward through the foothills of the Laguna Mountains to Ramona. Upon sighting the Army of the West and its slow moving column outside of Ramona, Gillespie ordered the Stars and Stripes "be given the breeze" to hearten the weary army troops. Gillespie had learned from his scouting party that he had sent out earlier that a large force of armed Californios were camped six miles west of Ramona at the Indian village in the San Pasqual Valley, just east of present-day Escondido. Gillespie passed this news to General Kearny, who immediately made plans to attack the enemy the next day. Being a horse-soldier, Kearny was excited about the chance of wiping out this Mexican army detachment and winning usable mounts for his own troops. Gillespie had his doubts about the battle-readiness of Kearny's force, and said so to the General.

"I read your report from Mexico City, Gillespie, on the inadequacies of the Mexican Army, and I'm prepared to wipe out these peons," said the General.

"But General, that is not the Mexican Army down in the valley, these are Californios!" Gillespie said.

"Better yet," replied the general, "just a bunch of cowboys with no military training. We will attack in the morning before first light."

"But General these are the sons and grandsons of Spanish military men who have taught their offspring well in military matters. They are considered the best horsemen in the world. I think you should reconsider your opinion of the enemy."

"Balderdash, Lieutenant! What do you, as a soldier of the sea, know about land warfare? We will attack as planned!"

The Spanish military forefathers of the Californios had taught their sons and grandsons well in horsemanship, military strategy, and the use of the fighting lance while travelling full speed on their small stallions. The Indian and Mexican vaqueros rode mounts that are similar to what are now called cutting horses. They are very fast, can stop on a dime, twirl and charge, all in one motion! At the start of the Mexican-American war in 1846, the Californios were considered some of the best riders in the world. Their counterparts in the U.S. Cavalry were no match at the Battle of San Pasqual.

That night the storm hit with full force. It doesn't rain often in California, but when it does the water comes down in buckets. December is usually the start of the rainy season, and 1846 was no exception. Luckily for Kearny, his group of men were camped just below the snow line, but they would still have to slip and slide their way down the hill before reaching the valley below. Even before the battle began, this would mean possible injury to some animals and troopers alike. It would be almost impossible to keep their weapons dry, but they did have their sabers. And a saber in the hand of a trained soldier was a lethal weapon.

As darkness fell over the American camp, Kearny decided to send a reconnaissance team down the hill to ascertain how many of the enemy he would face in the morning. Gillespie suggested that his "mountain men" from the California Battalion would be better suited for the job, as they could move with greater stealth. This idea was dismissed by Kearny, which was but one more of his mistakes.

The dragoon patrol snuck up on the enemy camp, but just at that moment, a dog started to bark which alerted the Californios. The patrol got away, but upon investigation by the Californios, a blanket was found marked "U.S. Army." The surprise was now gone!

Kearny decided to start the attack earlier than planned because the enemy had been alerted. At two-thirty in the morning of December 6, the long American column started the down-hill trek in the pouring rain. Gillespie had become irritated at Kearny's order that he and his men bring up the rear guard along with the baggage train. The Marine pointed out to Kearny that his field-gun and crew were in excellent condition, while the Army's howitzers were held together with rawhide and looked ready to fall apart at the first shot. Kearny reconsidered, then placed Gillespie's group near the front of the battle force. The dragoons, dazed with fatigue and chilled to the bone in the frosted remnants of their uniforms, could scarcely grip the reins of their mounts. Then it happened! The clouds parted, the rain stopped, and the moon shown bright, cutting through the darkness like a searchlight. The troops were able to make better time down the trail, as the pale dawn crept into the sky, however the typical California valley fog-after-a-rain began to form. Groping their way through the heavy mist, the Americans tried to make contact with the unseen enemy. Captain Abraham Johnston led the column onto the valley floor with twelve dragoons. General Kearny and Kit Carson followed with Captain Benjamin Moore and fifty dragoons, then came Gillespie and his San Diego contingent, followed by the howitzers. The pack train would bring up the rear. If the troops had any thought of using their carbines, it was quickly dismissed. The cartridges were swollen from the damp air, and it was near impossible to insert a percussion cap in the breech of the weapon. Most of the troops drew their sabers, others grasped their carbines as clubs.

As the forward contingent reached the valley floor, the fog started to lift a little, and General Kearny gave the order to, "Trot!" At that moment, Johnston spotted a number of Californios several hundred yards ahead. Johnston either misheard the order to "trot", or was carried away with the prospect of battle. Pulling his saber, he gave the order to, "Charge!," and galloped towards the enemy.

General and leader of the Californios, was Andres Pico. The seventy-five men under his command were ranchers, not soldiers, but their iron-tipped lances and superb horsemanship made them formidable cavalry. Pico had been told about Gillespie and his group leaving San Diego, as he had many loyal friends in the area acting as spies. What Pico didn't know, is the mission of Gillespie was to meet the Army of the West, he had assumed Gillespie was on a livestock search. Pico also assumed that Gillespie would make a circular tour, and not retrace his steps in returning to San Diego, but rather pass through the San Pasqual valley. The Californios had been waiting to ambush Gillespie, but now the scenario had changed with the finding of the U.S. Army blanket the previous evening. The sound of hooves and the clanking of heavy sabers in their scabbards were heard coming from the dark slopes above the valley. Pico's men were in the saddle with their lances ready and guns primed, waiting for the Americans as Johnston yelled the order to "charge!"

Californio General Andres Pico

General Pico had ordered his men to, "fire one shot, then use the lance", rather than reload. As Johnston's dragoons charged out of the mist, Pico's men stood their ground, aimed their weapons, and fired. The first shot caught Johnston in the head killing him instantly. The Californios then fanned out, sheathing their firearms, and tucking the lances firmly under their arms. Meanwhile, Moore's troopers had reached the level ground and continued the charge. Many were dropped from their saddles as the "lancers" went to work. Kearny and Gillespie were both wounded in the battle, but not fatally. Kit Carson survived without loss of blood, as a lancer lunged at him just as Kit's horse luckily stepped in a gopher hole, throwing Kit into the bushes.

After this first encounter with the Americans, Pico observed many more dragoons entering the field from the mountain trail. The sheer number of men, in those strange uniforms, had taken Pico by surprise. It was best to regroup and think this one out. The Californios galloped west down the valley on their superior mounts, stopping at what today is the entrance to the San Diego Wild Animal Park. The tattered condition of the enemy was obvious to Pico, who rallied his men and again swept down on the Americans. The dragoons and Gillespie's men were now scattered across the battlefield, operating not as a well-oiled military machine, but as individuals seeking survival. One sad note to this initial skirmish was that Gillespie's mountain men were not in military uniform and were easily mistaken for Californios by the dragoons. Several of Gillespie's men felt the wrath of the American saber, or wildly swung carbine.

Pico was still ignorant of the total force he faced, so he gathered his men and cantered away towards the west. The Americans had captured one prisoner. The number of dead or wounded Californios still remains a mystery, as Pico's men left no dead on the battlefield. The Americans with fewer than fifty men had come face to face with the enemy, but sixteen men and two officers were dead. Sixteen others were wounded; several of these would die before reaching the safety of San Diego.

Despite his wounds and the havoc wreaked on his army, Kearny at first wanted to chase after Pico, but thought better of it. The dead were strapped on mules, with sleds made to transport the wounded. Temporary command was turned over to Captain Turner who prepared a letter to Stockton advising of the situation. He asked for a force to meet them on the road to San Diego with provisions and transport for the wounded. One glaring error was made in the letter when Turner referred to "a very considerable Mexican force" and did not spell out the strength of the enemy. Four mountain men volunteered to take the letter to San Diego, and they made it without incident. Upon their return trip to San Pasqual with Stockton's reply, the Californios captured the four soldiers. Stockton had replied that wheeled transport for the wounded was in short supply, and that Gillespie had taken most of the horses and mules on the first mission. What really bothered Stockton was Turner's reference to "a considerable force" of the enemy. Stockton could not afford sending his Marines and sailors into a trap. The

Californios gained much needed confidence after the interception of Stockton's reply.

Kearny's men moved slowly westward, hugging the cart track close to the northern hillside of the valley. Kearny knew that Pico, given the chance, would attack in full force if the column moved through the level terrain of the river valley. As the column emerged from between two low-level hills, the Californios galloped up from behind, and started attacking the rear guard. The American wounded, along with the howitzers, were dragged to a small plateau half-way up the nearest hill, where boulders were rearranged forming a defensive position. The Army was safe for the moment, but trapped and starving. Their only hope was rescue by Stockton.

Time was on Pico's side. He was not about to charge up the hill into a hail of fire from one hundred entrenched soldiers. He could starve the Americans out, especially now that he had Stockton's reply.

That night, stringy mule meat was consumed by the troops, which gives the hill its name. Today, a national monument sits across the valley in Rancho Bernardo and gives the message that "Mule Hill" is just to the north.

The Army of the West faced possible annihilation. Another attempt to convince Stockton of the predicament had to be made. Lieutenant Beale of the Navy, who was Gillespie's second in command, along with Kit Carson and an Indian scout, volunteered to try and reach San Diego after darkness fell. Pico, anticipating a breakout by the Americans, had sentries posted on all three sides at the bottom of the hill. The volunteer group of three, in an attempt to be noiseless while slipping past the sentries, stuffed their boots into their jackets as they wormed downhill and across the valley. Upon reaching open country, all of the three discovered that they had lost their boots in the darkness. The next thirty miles would be very miserable with nothing but cactus, stones, and thorns the whole way to San Diego. Meanwhile Kearny, not knowing whether assistance from Stockton would be forthcoming, gave the orders to smash and burn all non-essential equipment in preparation for a breakout.

The three messengers split up in order to insure that at least one got through. The Indian arrived first, then Carson, then Beale with feet so bloodied that he had to spend a month recovering. Stockton was at last convinced of the peril facing the Americans. He immediately put togeth-

United States Marine Lt. Archibald Gillespie fires a 12 lb. Howitzer at charging Mexican Californios in Battle of San Pasqual, December 6, 1846. Illustration from a postcard. Painting by Colonel Charles H. Waterhouse, USMCR, Ret., for the US Marine Corps Art Collection.

er a force of 100 sailors and eighty Marines from the warships lying at anchor in San Diego Bay. He also included many of the ship's cannons.

Back on Mule Hill, December 10,1846, word was passed down from Kearny to his Army and Gillespie's men, that there would be a fighting breakout that next morning at first light. Throughout the early evening, each man took great pains in cleaning his carbine, and bringing his saber to a razor-sharp edge. The Army of the West was alert and tense, with not many sleeping during the cold, crystal-clear night. Suddenly, an alert sentry called out, "Halt, who goes there? Advance and be recognized." His voice carried in the clear air to the Californios camped below. In response to the challenge, a husky gruff voice shouted, "United States Marines!" A cheer went up throughout the American camp, and General Pico's men below the hill knew it was time to return home.

The Californios gave up on the idea for an independent territory, and accepted the status of being U.S. citizens. At least they had, along with the American help, thrown off the yoke of Mexico City, and would reluctantly accept statehood, which came several years later.

Epilogue to the Battle of San Pasqual

During the copper, bronze, and iron ages, the spear became more deadly, stronger, and sharper. The power of the spear became popular throughout Europe with the armored juggernaught on horseback, known as the medieval knight. With the invention of the gun and gunpowder in the late 1300s, the armored knight became obsolete along with the long lances of the cavalry and pikes of the infantry. These weapons were gradually replaced by the shorter and more effective saber. The Spanish retained the lance much longer than other European nations due primarily to their low cost and ease of manufacture.

The Spanish cavalry came to the Americas carrying a seven to ten-foot long wooden lance, tipped with a pointed iron head that was generally ten inches in length, and one and one-half inches wide. Halfway along the wooden shaft was a rawhide loop, which allowed the rider to sling the lance over his shoulder out of his way as he rode.

Upon the conclusion of the Mexican revolution with Spain in 1821, the Mexicans found themselves without money for new weapons or equipment; however, there was an abundance of old-fashioned and obsolete lances left over in the Spanish presidios.

As General Kearny found out, when his modern waterlogged carbines refused to fire, the old-fashioned lance was the weapon of the day. And after that day, the obsolete lance would pass into history, just like the bow and arrow which could not compete with a Winchester repeating rifle.

In the Battle of San Pasqual, the question persists: Why would a seasoned soldier, like General Kearny, attack an already alerted enemy, in the dark, on terrain that his foe was familiar with, and he was not? The answer could be many reasons, but in all probability, it most likely stems from the fact that Santa Fe was taken without a shot being fired. In Kearny's own experience, opposition at Santa Fe melted like snow in the desert, and blinded him to the possibility of any real resistance in California.

In terms of casualties, the Army of the West was dealt a crushing defeat at the hands of the Californios. In Kearny's many written reports to Washington, the victory was his, as the Californios had withdrawn from the field of battle. One entry that never was mentioned in the history books was the fact that Pico did pay a price for this battle. Eleven Californios died on the return to their ranchos when they were ambushed by the Luiseno Indians. This little known fact is referred to as the Pauma Valley Massacre.

In military conflicts, big and small, past and future, the first casualty of war always seems to be the truth. Thus a myth is born, and can be embellished many times over the years. Historians recognize early on that military and political leaders often justify their actions and decisions in published articles, autobiographies, or memoirs. Superior and overwhelming forces, incompetent subordinates, or the wrath of nature and its elements cause all lost battles. All great victories are the result of the leader's brilliant strategy.

A famous Chinese General, Sun Tzu, wrote a book twenty-four centuries ago, titled *Art Of War.* What he said many years in the past, was as true then, as it is today in modern warfare: "KNOW THE ENEMY, KNOW YOURSELF, AND YOUR VICTORY WILL NEVER BE ENDANGERED. KNOW THE GROUND, KNOW THE WEATHER, AND YOUR VICTORY WILL BE COMPLETE."

—Chapter Sixteen—

WAR IN THE BAJA

In the annals of California history, not much mention is made about the war for the Baja. Although the Mexican-American war in California ended in December of 1846, blood continued to be spilled in the Baja until the treaty was officially signed on February 2, 1848. Even then, hostilities continued for several more months.

During the war with Mexico the politicians in Washington erroneously concluded that there was just one California. That, of course, was true during the days of Spanish rule, but when Mexico declared its independence from Spain in 1821, the Mexican government had split the territory into two provinces: Alto California and Baja California. Some of the Washington politicos would correctly refer to "the Californias" in their speeches. Others interpreted that term to mean only "California" (the current American state.) Also adding to the confused terminology was the reference to "the Californios," the Mexican landowners who desired an independent republic, and "Californian," the term being applied to and used by newly arriving settlers in the territory. This linguistic confusion would ultimately lead to the division of upper and lower California between two sovereign nations: Mexico and the United States of America.

President Polk realized that it was necessary to occupy a territory before it could be claimed as a spoil of war. He sent United States Army troops from the New York Regiment south to the Baja towns of La Paz and Cabo San Lucas. These New York troops had just arrived in Santa Barbara after a long voyage around the Horn, and now they were ordered again aboard ship to take on permanent garrison duty in the occupation of the Baja.

During the early months of the war the American Pacific Naval Squadron had landed sailors and marines in several of the larger towns of the Baja, where the American flag was raised without much opposition. These troops would stay only a few days, and then continue their patrol of coastal waters aboard ships. It was felt that a regimental sized American occupation force was needed to exert territorial control.

President Polk, in his annual message to Congress on December 7,

1847 stated, "Baja California had been conquered by American arms and would never be surrendered to Mexico." The United States military, both Army and Navy, emphasized this point with the natives of Baja, many of whom gave aid to the American forces. Many of these people who had given their allegiance to the United States paid with their lives when Mexico regained control of the Baja.

In the latter part of 1847 and early part of 1848, the New York Volunteers were involved in a number of battles, and many lives were lost in the Baja while securing the area for the United States. At war's end, many of these United States soldiers of the New York Regiment deserted their posts. This desertion was caused by the fact that most of the officers of the regiment were regular army and they used severe discipline on the "volunteers." It was also a result of gold fever running rampant because of the discoveries up north. The deserters escaped punishment, in most cases, since their enlistment terminated automatically when hostilities were formally ended and peace restored.

Mounted dragoon and an infantry officer; painting by Charles McBarron

The main reason the United States lost the Baja was due to the "confidential and top secret" instructions from Secretary of State, James P. Buchanan, to the principal peace commissioner, Nicholas P. Trist. In these written instructions Buchanan wrote, "Whilst it is of the greatest importance to the United States to extend their boundaries over Lower California as well as New Mexico and Upper California, you are not to consider this as a "sine qua non" to the conclusion of a treaty. You will, therefore, not break off the negotiations if New Mexico and California can alone be acquired..." (Note the confusion of what constitutes "California.")

Five days after Trist left for Mexico, these "secret" instructions were printed in the Boston and New York newspapers. Because of this now public position, Mexico knew exactly how to proceed with negotiations of the peace terms and just how to stand tough on the Baja question.

A second set of instructions from Buchanan to Trist used the thirty-second parallel as a border, which cut the United States off from access to the Gulf of California. Buchanan wrote on July 19, "If Lower California cannot be obtained, then the line on the parallel of thirty-two degrees might be extended to the Pacific Ocean, taking care, in that event, to secure for our citizens, in accordance with your original instructions, in all time to come, a free and uninterrupted access to and from the ocean through the Gulf of California from and to their possessions north of the said division line."

The mouth of the Colorado River is below the thirty-second parallel, thus free access could only be obtained with Mexican approval.

We will learn in a later chapter about the exploits of William Walker and how this concern for access to the Gulf of California became of prime importance to those American people backing Walker and his crusade during the 1850s.

—Chapter Seventeen—

SIX FLAGS OVER CALIFORNIA

The histories of California and Texas have a number of similarities even though they are two entirely different areas. Texas has its cattle, its cotton, an ocean shoreline, several large rivers, snow and ice, many politicians, oil wells, theme parks, and numerous other attractions. California has all this and more; such as tall mountain ranges, below sea-level deserts, and redwood forests. Both states were acquired by war with Mexico, have a Hispanic background, and both were born in revolution.

"Six Flags Over Texas" is a well-known slogan, however California can also claim that distinction, even though very few of the state's populace can name the six flags that flew over this territory in the past.

The Spanish Flag flew over California from San Diego to Monterey from 1769 to 1821. This flag was replaced by the Mexican Flag in 1821 when Mexico gained independence from Spain.

During the Spanish rule, and unbeknown at first to the Spaniards, Russia raised their flag north of San Francisco at Bodega Bay and Fort Ross. The Russians also occupied the islands twenty miles off the entrance to San Francisco Bay. This made the Spanish and, subsequently, the Mexicans very nervous. General Mariano Vallejo was sent northward to establish settlements to act as a buffer at Petaluma and Sonoma. Later, John Sutter was allowed, as a non-Mexican citizen, to build a fort on the Sacramento River in order to halt any expansionist ideas held by the

Russians. In 1842, the Russians struck their flag and moved back to Alaska.

Meanwhile, American settlers were rattling their swords against the Mexicans, and marched in revolt on Sonoma, taking General Vallejo prisoner and in defiance raising the California Bear Flag. A few short months later, the Mexican War was declared, and upon its conclusion, the American Flag flew from every masthead and flagpole in the territory. When California became a state, its flag was designed to be similar to the one used in the Bear Flag Revolt, and now flies just below the American flag on all state buildings and institutions.

Not as many lives were lost in defending the six flags of California as were lost in Texas, nor did California merit as memorable a battle slogan as "Remember the Alamo!" but several notable battles did occur. Ironically, the majority of Californian lives lost were because two groups of independence fighters fought each other and not the Mexican Army which had returned to Mexico because of the war in Texas. We learned about the California Battle of San Pasqual in Chapter Fifteen, General Stephen Watts Kearny.

At dawn on June 14, 1846, the Mexican flag was lowered from the towering pole on the plaza at Sonoma, California. The replacement flag, showing a large star, a bear, and the words "California Republic," was soon fluttering in the breeze. Young children danced around the flagpole laughing and singing the words, "El Chancho! El Chancho!", which in Spanish means pig or shoat. Since the flag was a hurry-up job and hand painted in the few moments before the revolution, the picture of the bear had a strong resemblance to a pig. The banner of the Bear Flag Revolt would only be flown for a few weeks and then replaced by the stars and stripes.

William Todd designed the bear flag on a piece of unbleached cotton. The star imitated the lone star of Texas and the grizzly bear represented the many bears that inhabited California. The California state flag that was adopted by the 1911 state legislature used the Bear Flag as a model.

Several other flags have also been raised in California. John Sutter's New Helvetia Republic flag, California Mission Independencia bear flag, and Fremont's expedition flag also were displayed for brief periods of time in specific locations, but they did not represent "state-wide" movements.

Flags Important to California's History

Flags are symbols. They embody the ideas and ideals of the people who raise them. They make a bold statement to observers who are either opposed to or supportive of the cause represented by the flag. As such, it is important to categorize the flags that have flown over California, and to describe what they represented.

California was a Spanish protectorate from 1769 to 1821.

Russian influence over California lasted only thirty years, from 1812 to 1842, and was restricted to a single settlement north of Bodega Bay, now known as Fort Ross.

From 1822 to 1846, California was a province of Mexico, overseen by a succession of Mexican governors.

This flag represents the first attempt by the "Californios" to secede from Mexico. It flew briefly over Mission San Buenaventura.

The American Stars and Stripes at the time of California's admission to the Union. Note the 31 stars.

The current California state flag has elements similar to the Sutter flag, with the addition of a bear.

The "Revere Guidon" is believed to have been carried by the California Battalion in the Civil War. The original was destroyed in the San Francisco earthquake and fire in 1906.

The "Sutter Flag" flew over the state of New Helvetia, an independent state under Mexican protection. It is believed to be the precursor to the current California state flag.

The flag John Fremont carried on his topographical expedition into California. Note the twenty-six stars and stripes representing the United States and the eagle holding a "peace pipe," a symbol more easily recognized by the Native American Indians than the olive branch.

First Day Covers

A stamp is just a stamp until it is attached to a mailing piece, cancelled by the post office, and then delivered to its destination—so said a postal worker speaking with author, Tom Elliott. But the statement so intrigued Tom that he looked into this very different method of stamp collecting. He became enamored with the First Day Covers (FDCs) of artist, Fred Collins, and began collecting Collins' FDCs that deal with the history of the west and, in particular, those covers that portray important events in California history.

First Day Covers tell a story. An artist creates a picture, called a cachet, that usually mirrors a new-issue stamp from the U.S. Post Office. The stamps are themselves intended to honor or celebrate a person, date, or event important in United States history. The stamps are issued on a particular day (the first day of issue), affixed to the cover, and then hand-delivered to a selected post office for postmarking. They become collector's items because the stamp, cachet, and postmark all reflect ties to the event, person, or date being celebrated.

FDC illustrations used in this book are reprinted with permission of Fred Collins who, with a team of primarily four artists, have produced hundreds of FDCs over a period of two decades. More information about Fred Collins and his FDCs can be found in the book, *Hand Painted First Day Covers—The First 20 Years, 1978-1997,* published by James T. McCusker, Raynham, MA.

Collins
FIRST DAY OF ISSUE
Junipero Serra Museum
OLD TOWN PHILATELIC CENTER
AUG
22
1985
SAN DIEGO, CALIFORNIA 92110
Junipero Serra
USAirmail
44

California
1850
First Day of Issue
Collins
SACRAMENTO CA
SEP
8
2000
95813

WILDFLOWERS
CALIFORNIA
WILDWOOD, NJ
JUL
24
1992
USA
29
California Poppy

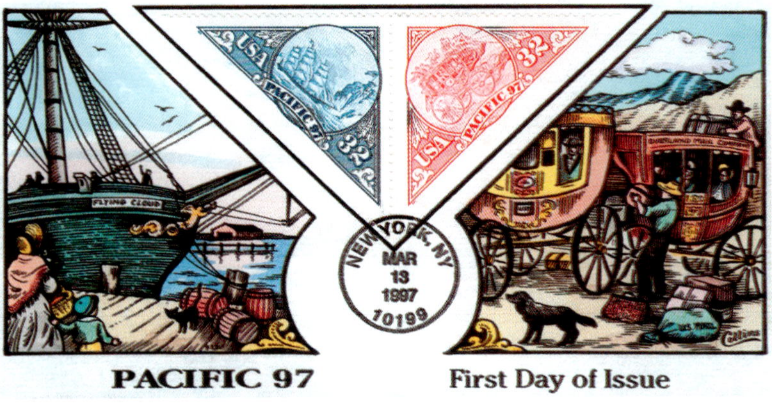
USA
PACIFIC 97
32
NEW YORK, NY
MAR
13
1997
10199
PACIFIC 97
First Day of Issue

1770
CARRETA
FIRST DAY OF ISSUE
AUGUST 30, 1988
SAN JOSE, CALIFORNIA
SAN JOSE, CA
AUG
30
1988
95101
Carreta 1770s
7.6 USA
FIRST DAY OF ISSUE
Nonprofit

CALIFORNIA
1850 First Day of Issue
SACRAMENTO CA
SEP
8
2000
95813

HOTEL
GRIZZLY FLATS SALOON
SHERIFF OFF
FIRST DAY OF ISSUE
AUGUST 25, 1987
TWAIN HARTE, CALIF.
GRIZZLY FLATS, CA
AUG 25 AM 1987
95636
Bret Harte
USA $5
BRET HARTE

KIT CARSON
29 USA
KIT CARSON
KIT CARSON, CO
OCT 18 1994
80825
Legends of the West

OFFICIAL FIRST DAY OF ISSUE
APRIL 14, 1982
WASHINGTON, D.C.
STATE BIRDS AND FLOWERS
WASHINGTON, DC
APR 14 1982
20066
FIRST DAY OF ISSUE
California
USA 20c
California Quail & California Poppy
CALIFORNIA POPPY
CALIFORNIA QUAIL
AUDUBON, NJ
APR 14 1982
08106
CALIFORNIA

Presidents of the United States

Four presidents who played prominent roles in America's westward expansion and California's admission to the Union are pictured here in Fred Collins' cachets.

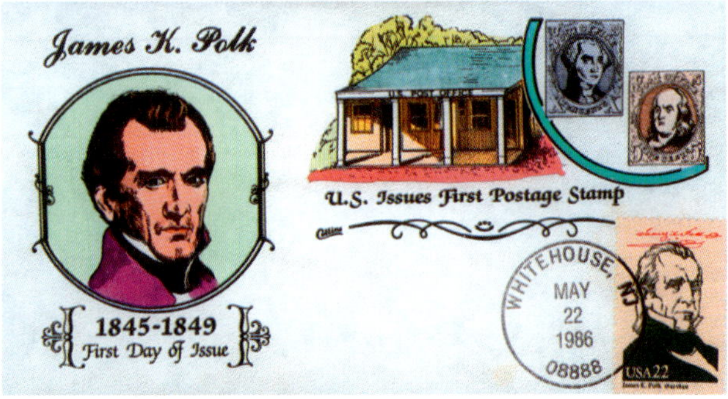

—Chapter Eighteen—

MINORITIES

During the period following statehood there were some 25,000 Chinese in California, making them the largest minority in the population. Mexicans, both those residing in California before the gold rush and those that had flocked to the gold fields after statehood, made up the second largest minority.

In some gold mining districts, three out of every ten people were Chinese—some were miners, some were laborers, and a large percentage were females. The women worked as cooks, cleaning personnel, and in other miscellaneous jobs, including prostitution. Many of the Chinese population became quite wealthy regardless of their occupation, despite the laws forbidding them from owning land or a business. The Oriental peoples, whether Chinese, Japanese, Korean, or Southeast Asia were hard working, frugal people. They worked long hours and spent very little money on luxuries, wanting to save what they did earn for future opportunities. Many of the oriental females, actually just young girls, had been brought to America and sold into sexual slavery as prostitutes. A good number of American miners, some just boys themselves, fell in love with and married these Chinese women, most of whom turned out to be loyal lifetime companions.

Illustration courtesy of California State Library.

Except for their language and accent the Mexican minority was hard to distinguish from Americans within the mining community. Most of the miners, whether American or Mexican, wore beards, were dirty, wore the same type of clothing, rode the same type of animal, smoked the same tobacco, and had deeply tanned arms and faces. Who could tell

How did these derogatory names arise? There are numerous myths concerning "Gringo" and "Greaser" but the most likely origins of the terms are as follows:

As the wagon trains rolled westward, especially on the southern route through the New Mexico Territory, many Mexicans were hired on as *vaqueros* to tend the cattle and other livestock. Upon reaching a stream or river, many of the wagons were floated across and a full day was spent on the other side "drying out." The wagon master would then always yell for the "greasers," and the hired hands would come forward, pull off the wheels of each wagon, dip their hands into large grease barrels and grease the axle hubs.

At night, around the smoldering campfires, these hardy travelers would entertain themselves by singing songs, the most popular of which included the words, "how green the grass grows." The Mexican *vaqueros* picked up on the words "green" and "grows" and would refer to the pioneers by combining the words, which became the slang term "gringo" meaning people from north of the border.

Whether these two myths are true is hard to prove; however, they are quite likely, as the wheels had to be greased almost daily, and the songs were sung every night.

the difference between "Gringo" and "Greaser?"

Another minority during the California gold rush was the Indians. During the Spanish exploration of California the Indians were actually in the majority with approximately 300,000 living in different tribes, mainly along the coastal areas and valleys. As the Spanish population increased the Indians were quickly outnumbered. Generally, the California Indian was peaceful and not on the warpath like the plains Indians east of the Rocky Mountains. Many became educated through the Spanish mission system and went on to become citizens active in both business and social life of the state. One example is Chief Solano of the Suisun Indian tribe:

Francisco Solano was the Christian name given to the Indian lad, Sem Yeto, when he was baptized at Mission Dolores in 1810. Sem Yeto in the Suisun Indian tribe language means "mighty arm," and a mighty arm was he!

General Mariano Vallejo, acting as Commandant of the North, established forts at Petaluma, Santa Rosa, and

Sonoma. During this building period, Vallejo and his men were subject to raids by the Suisun warriors. Requesting peace talks, Vallejo was amazed at the sheer power and grace of the powerful Indian leader. Sem Yeto, at six foot seven inches, towered head and shoulders above his Spanish-speaking enemy. The chief wore a simple loincloth, several strings of beads around his neck, and a headband with four large black and white feathers. During the talks both men learned to respect and trust each other, and later in life became very close friends. The title, "Chief Solano," was given to Sem Yeto by his *patrón*, General M.G. Vallejo.

Sam Yeto aka Chief Solano; illustration courtesy of G.P. Putnam & Sons, NY

In 1842 the Mexican government awarded a land grant, known as Rancho Suisun, to Chief Solano located in present day Suisun Valley, the ancestral home of Sem Yeto.

After California statehood, Vallejo became a member of the first Senate. He and Solano continued a close relationship, not only spending many a happy hour fishing and hunting at Rancho Suisun, but also both were active in representing and enforcing the treaties of the many Indian tribes throughout central California.

Women were also a minority in the gold rush days. The gold fields did not always require hard work and long hours. The miners often had free time on their hands to gamble, drink hard, and participate in other activities that would make their loved ones back east shudder with embarrassment. There were not a great number of women present in the early mining towns, and those who were came from many nationalities: the orient, Australia, South America, and some even from the eastern United States. A few of these women worked their own diggings hard for the glitter of gold, while others turned to the world's oldest profession, as they found it a lot easier to "work the men" for the gold dust and nuggets.

The females that had a talent for song and dance found that the miners were starved for entertainment and with pockets full of gold nuggets

In some history books the California Indians were referred to as "diggers," either derogatorily or as a slang term. Some believe that the name came about by the way the Indians maintained their food supply by digging in the ground for acorns, small edible animals, and even shellfish from the ocean. The name "digger," however, may have had a different source and may not be as derogatory as one is led to believe.

When Gaspar Portola came north from the California Peninsula on his exploration into Upper California, the first Indian tribe he encountered in San Diego was called the Diegueno. If that name is rolled around on the tongue in either English or Spanish it would not be hard to believe that "diggers" arose from the difficult pronunciation of the indigenous tribal name. Because of the many tribes, all with different names, throughout California, it was easier for the white man to refer to them all as "diggers."

When the first Spanish ship sighted what is known today as Santa Monica, the explorers called it, "The Bay of Smokes." Everywhere in the Los Angeles Basin, a cloud of smoke hung over the land, not much differently than the smog that currently occurs on summer days. What caused this smoke back in the late 1500's? There were no freeways, cars, buses, trucks, or other sources of pollution in the air that are common today. It was caused by the "diggers." The Indians in early California would clear a large area of brush and when the wind started blowing towards this cleared acreage, they would set fire to the remaining brush, causing small animals such as rabbits and rodents to run towards the cleared area. Using clubs and other weapons, the Indians would subdue the prey for their food supply. Sometimes the fire would get out of control and spread throughout the region, causing great clouds of smoke just as today's brush fires often spread during the dry season.

Fred Collins cachet #M1601

the miners were willing to share their wealth. Two very successful females—one an adult, the other a child—started on the road of fortune and fame in the town of "Rough and Ready" located near Grass Valley, north of Sacramento. Lola and Lotta became legends in their own time.

In 1854, a wagon pulled into town with Lola Montez, her husband, many suitcases and trunks, and a pet bear. The trunks were full of low-cut velvet gowns that had dazzled the kingdoms of Europe. Lola even claimed that she had once been the mistress to the King of Bavaria.

Lola and her husband bought a house in Grass Valley, and immediately began setting up a stage for their pet bear performance. Lola, in her velvet low-cut and revealing gowns, was an immediate success. Miners would journey many miles to take in the show and spend their gold dust. And it wasn't the pet bear they were interested in! Lola found that the life style in Grass Valley was not as glamorous as her days in Europe but exciting nonetheless. She returned home one day to find the pet bear shot through the head. Lola suspected her husband of this crime and after a lengthy fight, she asked him to move out.

Lola's immediate neighbors were the Crabtree family, whose seven year old daughter was named Lotta. Mrs. Crabtree was once quoted as saying, "Lola may have dazzled Europe, but she doesn't dazzle Grass Valley any longer. She still retains a slender, graceful figure, with black hair and the most brilliant flashing eyes I have ever beheld. But usually she was such a slattern that to me she was frankly disgusting. When attired in a low-necked gown as was her usual custom, even her liberal use of powder failed to conceal the fact that she stood much in need of a good application of soap."

Lotta Crabtree

After the demise of the pet bear, Lola found diversion in promoting the talents of her young neighbor, Lotta. She taught her protegé to sing and dance, and toss her golden curls. Little seven-year old Lotta Crabtree made her debut dressed in an Irish costume, dancing an Irish jig at the blacksmith shop in town to the accompaniment of a hammer on an anvil. Since most of the miners in this area were of Irish decent, the vigorous dance was deemed nothing short of sensational. Gold coins and nuggets covered the stage as little Lotta finished her dance. The tiny performer with her vivacious personality, merry laughter, and red-gold hair, went on to entertain in many gold towns as her career progressed. Later, she captivated crowds in San Francisco and New York. She became the toast of theater audiences for half a century. Lotta retired at an early age and lived a happy life until her death in 1924 at age 77. Each time that Lotta had performed, the stage was cluttered with gold coins, and when she died her estate was worth more than $4 million—all accumulated without a pick and shovel.

And what about Lola Montez? Having tired of Grass Valley and the other wicked mining towns in the gold fields, she packed her velvet gowns, laid flowers at the grave of the pet bear, and caught a ship for Australia. Little is known of her after she left for Australia, perhaps she returned to the King of Bavaria!

However, it would only be a couple of decades before women were no longer a minority, but were equally represented in the cultural, business, and social affairs of the state.

An interesting slang phrase still used to this day arose from the gold rush era: "Mabel, Mabel, off the table, the two bits is for the beer!"

Two bits or four bits, what today is slang for twenty-five or fifty cents, came from the miners in the California gold camps. Miners would carry gold dust in small sacks sometimes called "a poke." It was great when nuggets were found in the diggings, but generally when the earth was washed by panning for the gold, the process produced small slivers of the precious metal which was referred to as "dust." When this dust was used to buy supplies, equipment, or a beer or two, the merchant would state the price in "bits"—the miner would then open his poke and the merchant would reach in with thumb and forefinger and take a "squeeze" of gold dust (or a "bit"). Folklore says that saloon owners would always hire bartenders based on the size of their thumbs—the bigger the better!

It was also common knowledge in the gold camps that some bartenders would use "stick-um" on their fingers to increase the size of the "bit." Many saloon owners and bartenders became quite wealthy by the use of loose-fitting floor planks under the bar. Spilled gold dust would filter through the gaps in the planks and onto the bare ground below. Every week or so these enterprising entrepreneurs would sift the earth beneath their flooring, panning (like the miners) for the precious metal.

Photos from the Wells Fargo Museum

Every serious miner would also carry a pocket scale with which he could weigh the day's production of gold nuggets. His earnings for the day would be based on the value of $12 per ounce of gold.

It soon became evident that a system was needed for the production of gold currency or coins. Several private mints were established in San Francisco for the processing of gold and silver "slugs." The official U.S. Government mint would make gold and silver coins as well as the gold bar, used to transport the metal.

—Chapter Nineteen—

JAMES KING OF WILLIAM

A truly neglected and obscure character in California history was a man named James King. But this wasn't so back in the 1850s. What was California like before the arrival of James King of William?

Prior to the gold rush and its deluge of humanity that came from all walks of life, you could have traveled the 500 miles between Sonoma and San Diego without ever opening your wallet. The mission padres, as well as the owners of great cattle ranches, would welcome you with open arms. They would permit you to stay for weeks or even months, without charge, and if you did offer a piece of gold it would have been tendering an insult. In early California a man of honor did not accept payment in return for his hospitality.

Before the discovery of gold, California was a land virtually free of crime. There were very few jails, juries or courts, no sheriffs, no public hangman or executioners, no lawyers to prosecute or defend clients. During the twenty-seven years between 1819 and 1846 there were but six murders among white inhabitants of California. Houses were without locks and sea captains peddling their wares along the coast were content to return in a year or two to accept payment in produce. It was a good life, enjoyed by all.

Then the bombshell hit! Gold was discovered, and the sleepy little town of San Francisco with its population of 1,000 people burst at the seams. No tidal wave, no earthquake, no volcanic eruption could have been more devastating than what happened to San Francisco in the next ten years. At first, the area remained somewhat docile; one could still trust his neighbors, leave his doors unlocked, or leave his tools or merchandise unprotected. The flood of crime seemed to arrive overnight. Theft, murder, arson, robbery, and official corruption all made their appearance in the same year—the latter part of 1849. It wasn't just San Francisco, but all of California.

After statehood was declared, California became the paradise of rowdies, cutthroats, and white-collar bandits. The scum of the earth and cast-offs from all societies, as well as good people, swarmed to California. Scoundrels from British and Australian penal colonies and the dregs from our eastern states, mingled with the hard working pioneers all seeking the golden fleece. Pistols and Bowie knives became part of the required masculine equipment, as common as boots and hats. There was no law or order and it was no accident that San Francisco was devastated by fire six times in a year and a half. It was a common ploy of the gangs to burn one section of town and raid and plunder another section which had been left defenseless by those rushing to fight the fire. Even after the enactment of local and state laws, those citizens looking for refuge in the law were like sheep seeking protection in a den of wolves. What could they expect when the government office holders were the very scum of the community?

There were 1,200 murders in the city from 1850 to 1854, and during that time only one person was executed: a Spaniard found guilty of killing a Mexican. The word of the day was, "burn, loot, destroy, and kill. There are none that can stop you." The rewards for crime were much greater and easier than trying to eke out a living in the gold fields.

A vigilante committee was formed in early 1850 but it had no significant effect. It wasn't until one man alone dared to stand up to the establishment that any real order came to the town. His name was James King of William. San Francisco owes a lot to the memory of this man who did so much but received so little in return. There is little in the "city by the Golden Gate" to remind the current residents of this man's contributions.

James King was born in January of 1822, in Georgetown, District of Columbia. As James grew up, there were a number of others with the same name in town, resulting in the mail often going astray. To differentiate himself James added his father's name, William, as a suffix to his own surname.

James left home at age fifteen and spent a year in Pittsburgh working at odd jobs. He then traveled to Michigan where, in 1839, the rigors of the backwoods environment caused him to become sick. Returning to Pittsburgh, he worked as a postal clerk for several months and then joined a local newspaper. Little did he realize that journalism was to make his name memorable in future years. In 1841, at age nineteen, he abandoned journalism to become a bookkeeper in the banking business.

His elder brother, Henry, had been on two of Fremont's expeditions and had written to James regarding the wonderful opportunities available in Oregon. Leaving his wife and small children, King journeyed across the Isthmus of Panama in the summer of 1848 and waited in vain for a ship to bear him north to Oregon. King was not a gold-seeker, as news of the discovery had not yet reached the East Coast. Learning that it was easier to catch passage northward by going to Valparaiso, Chile, King caught a ship heading south.

When he reached that southern city in the shadows of the Andes Mountains, King learned that gold had just been found in California. Excitedly, he gave up on the idea of going to Oregon—the gold bug had bitten him! He immediately arranged passage on the next ship heading for San Francisco, arriving in November 1848. King didn't linger long in the city by the bay because he was off to the mines!

With pick, shovel, and pan he made his new home in "Dry Diggings" (later to be known as Placerville). James King of William was at the right place, at the right time, before the hordes of gold seekers hit "them thar' hills." With lots of luck and some elbow grease, King hit pay dirt. Within a few short weeks he had taken out enough gold not only to pay for all his supplies, but also for the entire trip expense, plus quite a little more to tide him over.

While in the mines he was sickened by all the gambling, rioting, and drinking that went on during the hours when the men were not working their claims. He would never again try to seek his fortune by means of a pick and shovel. He was off to San Francisco and the good life! Little did he know what a rough and rowdy city he was about to enter. His goal was to open a bank in San Francisco, but first he needed to take a voyage back east to secure capital for the new venture and return with his family.

When he returned from the east lady luck still smiled on James King as his bank became very successful. During the next few years he became one of the most prominent and wealthiest bankers of the far west. He had a successful business, a fancy carriage, and a fine home. This should be the end of the story; however, he was about to experience a downfall and, ultimately, his demise.

It all started when he became a member of the Committee of Vigilance in 1851. Then, in 1853, he was summoned to serve on a grand jury, which he did with great reluctance because it only paid $2,000 and that would hardly compensate him for the neglect of his business. The

Alta newspaper wrote on March 2, 1855 that, "James King of William has sustained a reputation for uprightness, fair dealing, and superior business qualifications. San Francisco does not boast a more quiet, courteous, dignified and honorable gentleman than Mr. King." This reputation was to serve King well during the days of adversity and financial strain that were soon to come.

A former cashier and now bank representative at Sonoma betrayed King's confidence by misusing a large sum of money sent to him for the purchase of gold dust. Without King's authorization or knowledge, the money was invested with the Tuolumne Hydraulic Association and became hopelessly tied up. Unable to meet his liabilities, King was forced to divest all of his property and even declined the protection of the bankruptcy act which meant that he lost his home.

In the 1850s everyone that had migrated to this remote land, so many miles from his or her original home, were starved for news. Ships bringing newspapers from the eastern seaboard were able to sell them out in the first five minutes after docking—and at the outrageous price of $1.00 each. Anyone that could lay their hands on a printing press instantly became a newspaper publisher, and San Francisco at one time had over 100 different newspapers being sold on street corners—some were daily, others weekly, while some were monthly. King's next venture after his bankruptcy was to become an editor for the *Daily Bulletin*, the vehicle of his future fame but also of his tragedy.

James King of William, while in his heyday of being a rich banker, had made an enemy or two along the way. One of these was Alfred A. Cohen, another very rich and prominent citizen of San Francisco. One day as they passed each other on Montgomery Street, heated words were exchanged as well as blows, and even though neither man was seriously hurt, Cohen several days later challenged King to a duel with pistols.

Dueling was actually against the law, but according to the code of the time, it was the honorable choice to accept the challenge. Numerous articles about duels would be reported in the newspapers, such as these that appeared in the *Alta Californian*:

> A duel was fought near the city on the morning of the thirteenth by Colonel William Walker and Mr. Carter, formerly of Sacramento. They used pistols—distance eight paces.

And similarly:

> Duels are becoming fashionable. Two occurred on the twelfth, one in the vicinity of the Mission Dolores, between two French merchants, and another at Contra Costa, also between Frenchmen. The weapons were small swords in both instances.

King found himself in a very awkward position. Duels were occurring continually; they were condoned by public opinion, and winked at by the officers of the law. They were fought not only by ruffians and gangsters, but also by the so-called respectable citizens, and newspapers gave them publicity. Would he be deemed a coward and weakling if he refused the challenge? He personally disapproved of the code, and so rather than take the easy road of acceptance, he chose the difficult road of refusal. The following is his response, sent to and printed by all newspapers of San Francisco. It is addressed to Cohen's "second," who had delivered the challenge to King.

> Mr. John K. Hackett
>
> Sir: I now proceed to give you my reply to the note you handed me last night, and first, waiving other insuperable objections to the mode indicated of settling such difficulties, I could not consent to a hostile meeting with Mr. Cohen. The public have already been fully advised of my estimate of his character. The relative position of Mr. Cohen and myself are entirely unequal in worldly fortune, and domestic relations. He is understood to be possessed of an abundant fortune. In the event of his fall, he would leave ample means for the support of his wife and child.
>
> Recent events have stripped me entirely of what I once possessed. Were I to fall, I should leave a large family without the means of support. My duties and obligations to my family have much more weight with me than any desire to please Mr. Cohen or his friends in the manner proposed. I have always been opposed to dueling on moral grounds.
>
> Whilst nothing could induce me to change my principles on the subject of dueling, my conscience is perfectly easy as to my

> right and the propriety of defending myself should I be assaulted.
>
> Do not flatter yourself, sir, that this communication is made out of regard either to yourself or to Mr. Cohen. I write this for publication in the newspapers. I avow principles of which I am not ashamed, and shall abide the result.

As stated earlier, the people of San Francisco as well as those in the rest of the state were starved for news, and they would read every word of their newspaper. The article from James King was no exception and letters of sympathy and approval poured in daily. The majority of newspapers endorsed his stand with admiration for his moral courage and sound principle. By his refusal to accept the challenge, they tendered their thanks for his bold, manly, and uncompromising manner. A movement was launched to make dueling in California illegal. There is no way to measure how many lives this saved from a cruel death or how many families he rescued from bereavement. James King of William was truly a hero of the day in the eyes of all the citizens.

On the eighth of October 1855 the *Daily Evening Bulletin* was launched. The publisher was C.O. Gerberding with James King, editor. Gerberding had agreed to give complete editorial control to King whose goal was to strike at evil and corruption within the state, and in particular within San Francisco. James King would use a mighty pen in the weeks to follow. He not only wrote about ballot-box stuffing, corruption of officials, payoffs, organized crime, and deeds against the honest citizens, but he also named names, which made for a widening circle of enemies. King wasn't running a popularity contest, he was already the most popular man in the city. If he had been a dueling man, the chance had come up more than once for an acceptance to a life-or-death encounter. The paper grew at an astronomical rate, and within two months its circulation had surpassed all rival journals in the city. On April 5, 1856 (a little more than a month before his assassination) the following article appeared in the *Bulletin*:

> Were we to resign the post as Editor of this paper, we should be ashamed to walk the streets of San Francisco. There is not a man, women or child, from Shasta to San Diego, who would not say that we had been bought off. Gentlemen, you have not gold

> enough in your vaults, nor is there enough in the hills and gulches of the State to buy us! We have been wealthy, and know the uses of money; but in our poverty we have learned practically that there can be more real happiness in the poorly furnished cottage than in the most magnificently furnished apartments. We would not exchange the hearty welcome of the mechanic and the laborer and the honest merchant for all you can offer.

King had steadfastly resisted all attempts by his adversaries to silence him, buy him out, or otherwise secure a controlling interest in the paper. His slogan was, "It's no use trying to dodge the *Bulletin*, gentlemen!"

Editor James King of William was daily gambling with his life, as his enemies became more and more menacing. Credit will not be given to the man, James P. Casey, that fired the fatal shot, except to say that he was a very wealthy and prominent politician and ex-convict. King had written about Casey's election as supervisor from a district from which he was not even a resident. King also stated that Casey was not the only politician to have come to prominence while under the shadow of eastern penitentiaries. The fateful day that this article appeared, May 14, 1856, Casey walked into King's office where a heated verbal battle took place. An hour later, after throwing Casey out of the office, King locked up and headed for dinner. Down the block stood Casey. As King approached, Casey threw back his cloak and drew a pistol. It was all over in a matter of seconds.

James King of William

King didn't die immediately, in fact, several passers-by rushed to his rescue and quickly secured medical aid. After a time his condition, although critical, appeared to improve somewhat. It wasn't until six days later that James King of William took his last breath.

Meanwhile Casey, being the confident assassin, did not realize he was taking any great risk by shooting his victim in broad daylight. The city was so entrenched in lawlessness, that most thieves and murderers felt that they would be well protected by the authorities, but Casey lost his confidence as a large mob surrounded him yelling, "Kill him! Kill him!"

Casey was rescued by the friendly police and rushed to the nearby station house, but pandemonium had already broken out in the streets of San Francisco. The mob stormed the station house as Casey was ushered out the back door and rushed by carriage to the county jail, some blocks away. The mob frenzy continued day and night as James King lingered on his deathbed. The military were called in but lacked the numbers to control the multitude of irate citizens. This storm of popular emotion continued with no sign of subsiding throughout the next few days.

San Francisco—Shame on you! There are streets named in honor of Sutter, O'Farrell, Jackson, Clay, Larkin, Montgomery. There is even a Bush Street-but King? The only King Street in the city is at the end of the Embarcadero, in the industrial area below the Oakland Bridge. It runs for about seven blocks. It is certainly not a prominent way to say "Thank You" to one of your city's finest historic citizens. However, there is also no Casey Street. At least in that omission there is a modicum of good taste and respect.

The Vigilance Committee from 1851 was reactivated and soon had over 2,600 members. It was not organized as a mob, but as a "government within a government," the sole purpose to combat certain abuses in the administration of justice. They marched towards the county jail with military precision, and demanded the sheriff give up Casey to stand trial.

At noon May 20, 1856 James King of William expired. At the same moment a verdict was being handed down on James P. Casey—"GUILTY! DEATH BY HANGING." The city mourned the loss of their beloved leading citizen as though he was a president or an emperor. The *Daily Bulletin*, on the twenty-third, wrote the following about the burial procession:

> As it defiled solemnly along Washington and Montgomery streets, its ranks were rapidly augmented by horsemen, footmen, and carriages, until there seemed to be no end to the mournful cortege. Certainly not less than 25,000 persons witnessed the scene and participated in the honors paid to the dead. It is impos-

> sible to say with any certainty how long the procession really was. It must have extended greatly over a mile and possibly reached a mile and a half. Nor was it composed of any one class of our fellow citizens, or of any one nation. Every trade, avocation and profession was represented, and natives of almost every clime were marching in its ranks. Silently, thoughtfully, mournfully, they walked behind the corpse—strangers, most of them to his person while living, but friends of the principles he advocated, and mourners now at his funeral. Even the lowly African was there, trudging along with tearful eyes and saddened heart, for he remembered that Mr. King when alive pleaded most eloquently for all who were oppressed, poverty-stricken and unfortunate.

It was ironic that on the very hour that King's body was being conveyed to rest that his slayer was reaping the penalty of his crime.

—Chapter Twenty—

THE GRAVEYARD OF SHIPS

There are actually two ship graveyards located in California. One is located in Suisun Bay off of Benicia, where a great number of Victory and Liberty ships left over from World War II and Korea are tied side-by-side, row-upon-row, and anchored in the middle of the bay. This is called a "strategic storage area" in case the ships are needed for any future national emergency.

The Sacramento River enters San Francisco Bay at this point in the Suisun Bay. So what is the importance of that fact? The fresh water run-off from the Sierra Nevada meets the salt waters of the Pacific Ocean at this point of the bay and effectively prevents barnacle growth.

Now let us explore the second "graveyard of ships." Actually, the whole unfriendly coastline of California has seen the demise of many ships over the centuries, but one spot has seen more than its

Barnacles have always been the scourge of ships that sail the oceans of the world. The build-up on the ship's bottom can drastically cut down on the speed and handling of the vessel—and speed is money! In the old days of wooden ships and canvas sails, a nice level beach was always welcome when it came time to "scrape the growth." The ship would be grounded on the beach at high tide, then secured to a tree on shore. During the low tides, the ship would be careened in order for the sailors to scrape the barnacles. Sometimes this job would take several weeks to complete. A good example of this is the voyage of the Golden Hind, captained by Sir Francis Drake, when he explored the Bolinas Bay area. It's too bad he missed the entrance to San Francisco Bay in the fog, as he could have taken advantage of the fresh water from the Sacramento River, and the barnacles would have fallen off.

Illustration courtesy of Doubleday, NY

share—Point Pedernales, a point of land that extends seaward halfway between Los Angeles and Monterey. Many maritime disasters occurred here on this fog bound, California coastline. The worst incident occurred at 9:00 p.m., September 8, 1923. Nine fleet destroyers of a U. S. Navy squadron, through navigational error, "turned left" before they should have. Actually, two of the destroyers veered off at the last moment before running up on the rocks, and missed all the excitement. The squadron was running full bore in a follow-the-leader exercise and were "close hauled" with very little clearance between them. At two-minute intervals, each of the seven ships ran up on the rocks in what would be one of the worst naval tragedies in United States history.

In the gold rush heyday of California, there were no trains, airplanes, trucks, or other modern modes of transportation, just horse-drawn stagecoaches and wagon trains. With the advent of large gold shipments leaving San Francisco for New York, the only sensible means of transport was by sailing ship. There were plenty of these available since most of the crews had abandoned ship in San Francisco Bay in order to strike it rich in the mother lode country. The ships' owners had doubts about the trustworthiness of the few officers and sailors who were still available. Lloyds of London would insure the vessel for pennies on the dollar of its value; however, it was up to Wall Street investors to insure the cargo. A number of ships that sailed were never heard from again. It was assumed that while approaching Panama, a mutiny had taken place and the voyage continued to unknown parts of South America. The gold would then be off-loaded, the passengers killed, and the ship scuttled. An alternative assumption was that Mother Nature had taken her toll on these ships.

Most of the California coastline is facing westward including all the "safe harbors," bays, and beaches. Mother Nature at times can be cruel as Pacific Ocean storms can funnel and slam these half-moon shaped areas. Many a ship has been lost due to these storms that pound ashore, usually during the winter months, even while the ship is safely at anchor in what is felt to be a "protected environment."

It was not always the blast of winter that sank ships while at anchor, but Mother Nature would also send an occasional "monster wave" that would drive ships high onto the beach or rocks of the coastline.

In researching early Pacific Ocean shipwrecks, I found as the cause

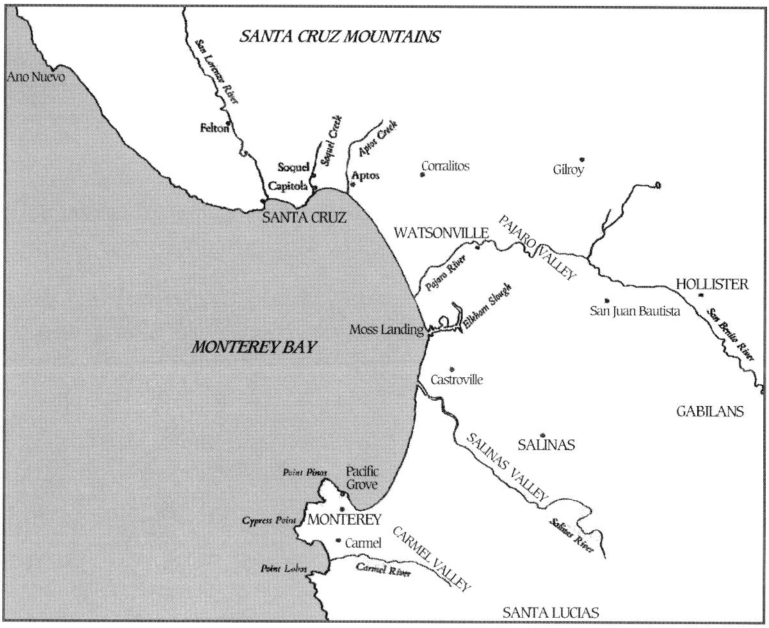

California's bays and harbors generally face westward.

of many of these misfortunes the listing of "monster wave." It reminded me that during the summer months of my teenage years, long ago, I would trek to Neenies Beach in Santa Monica to surf and play volleyball. The lifeguard station and platform was just beyond the high-tide line where it was safe from the wave action. One day I arrived and found debris littering the beach (mainly seaweed, fish, rocks, and large gravel) all the way to the main road. The usually dry sand was completely wet with many puddles. The lifeguard stand was floating in the surf. I asked the lifeguard, "What happened?" His response was, "Monster wave hit last night—must have been at least sixty-foot!" Now as a surfer, I knew that anything between three-foot and six-foot was the norm—I just couldn't visualize a wave that big!

You may ask yourself, "What causes a monster wave?" The answer is an earthquake. I don't mean a California quake, but one that occurs many thousands of miles away in Japan or Alaska. The early day sailors didn't have advance notice of the quakes occurring, like we do today, so one moment could be peaceful, and the next moment might find them swimming for their lives.

An example of a tidal surge from a personal experience is one I had in the late 1950s when I was living in San Rafael, California. There was a quake in the Aleutian Islands of Alaska and a small wave was created heading south and eastward. The harbor at Crescent City, California took the full brunt of the action as the wave continued southward toward San Francisco. In the movies, tidal waves are shown as being huge mountains of water moving across the surface of the ocean. Actually, the wave moves through the water and is only a few feet in height. It is when the wave approaches a coastline that water surges to create what is called a tidal wave. It is usually the surge inward that causes damage. In the case of the well-protected Bay of San Francisco, water ebbed seaward through the Golden Gate, then came roaring back into the Bay. At the San Rafael yacht basin, the water had left the channel leaving boats high and dry on the muddy floor. As the water, which had been sucked out, came rushing back, many boats became piles of floating splinters and pieces of junk. It was reported that a Coast Guard twin-screw cutter damaged its propellers on the floor of the bay as the water began the outward flow.

Another example of damage caused by an earthquake thousands of miles away is Hilo, Hawaii. As the small wave passed through the ocean approaching Hilo, the outgoing tide exposed many parts of the beach never seen before. People raced out to collect souvenirs from the sea floor. Then the wave and surge hit with a fury, killing hundreds. The wave continued inland, and didn't stop until half of Hilo had been destroyed.

The heavy storms, tidal surges, waves, or even sea monsters that threaten the lives of those who traverse the sea should be enough—but pirates were also a factor in early California. They would raise distress signals on their ship and then board the treasure ship when it responded, kill the crew and passengers, and transfer the booty to their own ship before again scuttling the evidence and victims without a trace. It would be just another case of a ship "lost at sea." These ruffians would sometimes headquarter on Catalina or Coronado Island awaiting their prey. They found this work of the devil much easier than digging and washing sand for sixteen hours a day in the gold fields.

When leaving San Francisco by sea, a ship would sail due south until the coast of California curled to the east. Making a turn to the left, or port, the ship would then steer a southeasterly course. This route can easily be seen by looking at a map of California, Mexico, and Central America. If the ship didn't turn, and continued on a due south heading, it would be several thousand miles west of Panama, thus extending its journey by a week or so depending on the winds. While making the southeasterly turn to hug the California coast, the ship would be dangerously close to the Channel Islands off Santa Barbara, giving the pirates an excellent chance to snare their prey.

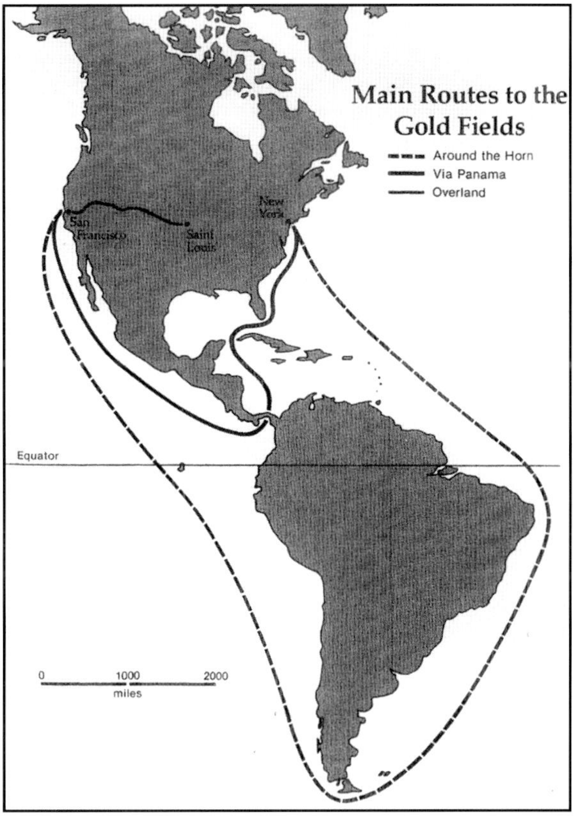

Illustration from California History, *Harlan Davidson, IL*

Fog, currents, wind, and adverse weather, along with human error in navigation, could all lead to problems for a ship's captain. Sometimes human lives, in addition to cargo and vessels, were lost even without the presence of pirates.

One of the finest inventions of the period was the ocean going steamship with side wheels or steam propellers. The pirates with their sailing ships didn't stand a chance against these mammoth ships that not only could go forward, but also backward, and could turn on a dime. During the late 1840s a number of these steamships were built on the east coast and used for the Atlantic trade to Nicaragua and Panama. Others were sent around the "Horn" for the Pacific trade. By 1854, there were over twenty-two of these vessels operating between San Francisco and Central America. The most famous one, was the S.S. YANKEE BLADE.

There were others that had very short service periods. The S.S.

UNION left San Francisco on July 1, 1851 en route to Panama. On July 5, she ran onto an outer island at Rosario, which is sixty miles south of San Quentin in lower California. All of the 250 passengers, their luggage, and a treasure of $300,000 in gold were brought ashore safely. The S.S. NORTH AMERICA ran aground seventy miles south of Acapulco on February 28, 1852 and had to be replaced by owner Cornelius Vanderbilt. The S.S. PIONEER was lost in August 1852 at St. Simon's Bay (San Simeon) before she completed her first trip to San Francisco. The S.S. INDEPENDENCE ran aground off the southern tip of Margarita Island and burned with the loss of 130 passengers. Four weeks after the accident, a small schooner arrived at the island to take on the 280 surviving passengers. On April 10, 1853 the S.S. LEWIS missed the approach to San Francisco Bay during a heavy fog. Continuing northward ten miles, she struck the Duxbury Reef at the entrance to Bolinas Bay. No life was lost in this accident, but the ship was destroyed.

Edward Mills owned the S. S. YANKEE BLADE. He was a staunch Yankee and applied Yankee names to all his vessels. Fancying himself as a "ladies' man" (who in those days people called a "dandy" or "blade"), Old Ed applied the name YANKEE BLADE to his new vessel.

Steamship racing was not uncommon on the waters of the Pacific, but did cause concern in many circles. Due to the stiff competition between the various steamship companies primarily in the lowering of passenger rates, Ed Mills and Cornelius Vanderbilt decided to join forces and form a partnership. Vanderbilt had promised Captain Randall, of the YANKEE BLADE, a sizable bonus each time he beat the fourteen-day dash to Panama.

The main competition for Vanderbilt was the Pacific Mail Lines and their steamship the S.S. SONORA. The first trip to Panama, made by the YANKEE BLADE, was uneventful, but the second trip was almost a disaster. Captain Randall really wanted that bonus and was almost a day ahead of the SONORA when he ran out of coal 300 miles short of Panama. Anchored off Coiba Island, Randall sent up distress rockets but the SONORA ignored the signal, and went on to win the race. A steam tug was sent from Panama to rescue the BLADE from its dilemma, however Randall had put ashore several crew members and passengers to chop down some trees for fuel, and the BLADE steamed into the harbor before the tug got underway.

The YANKEE BLADE, having returned to San Francisco, was now preparing for its third trip to Panama. She carried a crew of 122 officers and men, in addition to 812 "listed passengers." A number of stowaways were hidden in the bowels of the ship, and the estimated total number of passengers, crew, and stowaways, was close to 1,200 people. Included with the stowaways was Jim Turner, and his "band of bad guys." A grand jury had twice convicted old Jim of assault with deadly weapon, and he was on his way for a long stay in the local jail when he escaped.

The day before sailing, many advertisements appeared in the various newspapers by people wanting to bet on the outcome of ships' arrivals. One ad stated that $5,000 would be wagered that the passengers of the YANKEE BLADE would arrive at Panama before those of the SONORA.

The owners of the SONORA, upon seeing this ad, immediately contacted the ship's captain, R.L. Whiting, and told him in no uncertain terms that he had specific orders to not engage in any racing.

On the sunny afternoon of Saturday, September 30, 1854, four ships were ready to depart San Francisco. The S.S. YANKEE BLADE and S.S. SONORA were both headed for Panama. The S.S. GOLIAH was headed for San Diego, and the S.S. CORTES for Nicaragua. In leaving the harbor, Captain Randall took his place astern of the GOLIAH, followed close behind by the SONORA, then the CORTES in fourth place. As they passed through the Golden Gate and reached the open sea, Captain Randall stopped his engine allowing the SONORA to catch up. As the two ships aligned themselves, bows pointed southwest, Captain Randall lowered the ships flag as a traditional signal of challenge. The SONORA dipped her ensign in acceptance. Both ships lurched forward, churning up the water with their huge side paddles. The race was on!

After about twenty-five miles, a thin fog was encountered, and Captain Randall gambled that Captain Whiting of the SONORA would reduce speed. He was right, as the YANKEE BLADE surged ahead. He soon lost the SONORA in the fog astern. About twenty-two hours out of San Francisco, Captain Randall ordered a course change to southeast by south and he reduced his speed to between ten and twelve knots per hour. The fog was getting heavier, and by dead reckoning, the captain assumed the ship's position was twenty miles or more seaward off the coast. The key phrase here is "or more," because twenty miles doesn't cut it! The Channel Islands, particularly Catalina, are all from five to twenty miles off the coast, and more leeway should be given these unmovable water hazards. The "left turn" to a southeasterly direction, especially in fog, should never be attempted on the Southern California coast until the ship is about even with the Mexican border. When Captain Randall made his turn, a passenger came into the wheelhouse, a sea-faring man himself. His name was Captain Henry Ansley. Captain Ansley told Randall that he had spotted land dead ahead through the spotty fog. Randall said, "There is nothing to worry about, we are in good shape." A few minutes later, at exactly 3:30 p.m. on October 1, 1854, a grinding crash was felt throughout the ship. The bow lifted skyward and the ship came to an abrupt halt. The land that Henry Ansley had sighted was still a quarter-mile ahead; however, the ship had ridden up on a barely submerged rock pinnacle. This rock fang, a reef-like ledge, had impaled the ship and tore a sixty-foot gash in the wooden bottom. Both anchors were quickly dropped in order to keep the vessel from sliding to a watery grave.

Drawing by A. T. Harrison, Yankee Blade Passenger; from www.mms.gov

There was pandemonium throughout the ship. It was at this point that Jim Turner and his cutthroats sprang into action. Well armed with pistols, knives, and weapons that they had smuggled aboard they proceeded to break into every cabin, robbing the passengers of their valuables. Much of the hard-earned gold from the mother lode passed into unfriendly hands that afternoon.

Captain Randall set off in a small boat with four crew members to search for a safe place to land the passengers. Prior to leaving the ship, express orders were given to make ready the other boats, with women and children only, but not to launch any boats until the captain returned. There were very few landing spots on this rocky coastline. Only one was found after an hour's search. Randall, upon returning to the ship, was very upset to find the boats lowered and proceeding to shore against his orders.

In the captain's absence the ruffian gang had found the keys to the liquor cabinet in the ship's bar and became drunken and unruly. They stationed guards at gangway and lifeboat locations to keep the passengers from leaving the ship. A good number of these villains, including Jim Turner, commandeered several of the boats, and loaded them with stolen valuables.

The official price of gold in the 1850s was $20.67 per ounce established by Congress in 1837. When miners hit "pay dirt" they were reluctant to leave the gold fields, so they would sell the gold to traders at $12.00 per ounce. The trader would then transport the gold to a private mint and receive $17.00 per ounce. The profit would pay for the trader's risk in transporting the valuable cargo. The difference between the price paid by the mint and the official price offset the refining of impurities in an ounce of raw gold, plus gave a profit to the mint. The refined gold was then made into coin or bars by the mint. The most popular bar was the small two-pound bar (24.24 troy ounce) valued at $500 each. A good number of these gold bars could be carried in a money belt with relative ease.

Jim Turner and his band of pirates headed for shore, all laden down with money belts. When they reached the heavy surf several boats were swamped causing most of the villains to drown. The moral of this story: don't try to swim with somebody else's gold!

In the months and years that followed this tragic event, many descriptive and vivid accounts were written to newspapers. Sketches, drawings, and paintings were made of the disaster, as well. Captain Horace Bell, a California Ranger, was a passenger aboard the rescue ship S.S. GOLIAH, and he authored a book entitled *Reminiscences of a Ranger* in 1881. The following is an excerpt from his book that gives a pretty good idea of the heroism that took place off desolate Point Pedernales so many years ago—some of the most dangerous but successful nautical feats in the history of seamanship were performed by Captain Salisbury Haley.

> Haley commanded the Goliah, a staunch craft, now, in 1881, doing good service on Puget Sound. She first kissed the briny deep at the mouth of the Mississippi, in 1846, having been built

for a tow-boat of great power. The Goliah carried a few passengers, among whom were Aleck Bell, the author, Captain Burt, a man of nautical note at the time, also Charley Mathews, John Brannan, John McMullen, and a party of adventurers, mostly Texans, armed *cap-a-pie*, and on their way as a pioneer prospecting party to Arizona. If I am not mistaken, Grant Oury was of the party. We sailed past the Golden Gate at about four o'clock having been preceded about six hours by the great Pacific Mail Steamship Company's steamer, Sonora, and the Yankee Blade, an opposition steamer with about 1200 passengers. This was in October, '54.

We steamed beautifully on our way all night, stopping at way ports during the day, and early on the second morning ran into a heavy fog bank, and were feeling our way along carefully, when all at once we heard the roar of breakers close on our port quarter, which created quite an alarm. Haley at once commenced to change our course more to starboard, when, above the roar of the breakers, which was not heavy, we heard the cry of a thousand human voices for help. It seemed as though we were rapidly nearing the breakers and the place from whence proceeded the cries for help. In a few minutes we were headed off from the roar of the breakers and the sounds of human woe. Nothing is more solemnly terrifying than to be on shipboard near the breakers and in a fog bank, but add to this the knowledge of being in close proximity to a wreck is awe added to terror, and is paralyzing to the bravest heart. About the time we were headed off, the fog lifted almost as perceptibly as the raising of a curtain, and lo! within a cable's length lay a large steamer, which proved to be the Yankee Blade, a hopeless wreck, her deck swept by the the breakers and the hundreds of passengers in the rigging, on the roofs and bridge, clinging to the rail and shrouds, presenting one of the most awful pictures one can well imagine. The sea was comparatively smooth, yet the swell was heavy and the breakers were rough.

The wrecked steamer lay considerable distance from the shore, head on, having settled on a sunken rock which pierced her bottom amidships, on the northwest side of Point Arguello, the most northern point of Point Concepción, and had struck at about midnight. She was many miles out of her direct route, which at the time was ascribed to one of two causes—one was a great variation in the magnetic needle caused by a supposed local attraction, and the second that a crowd of organized roughs had taken passage on board the ill-fated steamer with intent to beach and rob her, there being the regular bi-monthly shipment of one and a half million or more dollars in gold dust, besides that carried by the passengers; that the roughs had surreptitiously changed the compass, which caused the stranding of the steamer as we have found her. This last proposition was supported by the fact that as soon as the steamer settled, the roughs first broke into the store-room and captured the liquors, and then commenced the pillage of passengers, many of the crew uniting with the roughs. They also possessed themselves of the boats, and when sufficient gold had been secured, was placed in a boat manned by them, and started for the shore.

The boat swamped in the breakers and the pirates and their gold went down together. The others of the steamer's boats were lost in the same manner, until but one small boat of capacity to carry a half dozen people at a time remained. The stern of the Yankee Blade had settled to thirty feet below the water level and her head had raised correspondingly high, so that her deck line was at an angle of about forty degrees. The wounded monster labored heavily and was liable at any moment to break in two amidships. It was a marine impossibility to approach her with a boat in the ordinary way, and Captain Haley resolved upon a plan that seemed original and extremely dangerous to his own vessel, and as expressed by many seamen on board at the time, as most certain to insure the destruction of the Goliah.

When remonstrated with on the fool-hardy venture, Captain Haley said: 'It is the only possible way to save those unfortunate people. There are over a thousand of them while there is less than a hundred of us, and if they are lost then we will go together.' The plan adopted and carried out was as follows: the Goliah being headed off backed in as near the wreck as deemed safe, and a buoy was attached to a line, dropped overboard and drifted to and was secured and drawn on board the Yankee Blade, to which was attached the ship's great hawser, which, in turn, was hauled on board the Goliah, and when safely secured steam was turned on and the hawser was drawn taut, then the anchors of the Goliah were carried ahead and cast, and heaving ahead on the windlass, as well as the steam propelling force, drew that hawser as taught as a fiddle string.

The next thing was to swing one of the Goliah's boats by loops to this hawser, attach a line to one end of the boat, float

S.S. Goliah attempts rescue of S.S. Yankee Blade (original painting)

the end of the line on board the wrecked steamer, by which the boat was drawn over, sometimes being suspended high above the water, and having another rope attached to her she was drawn back to the Goliah laden with living freight. And Oh! such freight as come off in the first few trips of our hammock-like craft. The roughs had full control on board the unfortunate craft, and were the first to be saved. Haley roared through his trumpet to the captain of the Yankee Blade, "Send the women and children off first." Still the roughs must be thinned out before the officers could control the debarkation. In an hour one hundred roughs were on board the Goliah, and the women and children commenced to cross the bridge in a lively manner, and soon it became necessary to commence to dispose of our accumulated cargo of living freight. The two remaining boats of the Goliah having found a safe landing place, now commenced to remove the accumulating cargo to the land; for bear in mind, reader, the Goliah was, as compared with the wrecked monster, a mere launch. Up to this time, however, the Goliah's people had not heard of the roughs and their piratical acts on board the Yankee Blade. However, those who had come on board took possession of the cabins, including the ladies', and when requested by Captain Haley to vacate in favor of the rescued women and children informed him that they had commanded "the Yankee Blade and while on board the Goliah would do as they thought proper." Haley remonstrated with them in vain, and being informed by a lady passenger of their character and doings on board the wreck, took a most decided step to subject them to absolute control. In the meantime the sea rolled, and the staunch old Goliah, God bless her, strained, groaned and writhed in agony as a living victim when stretched upon a rack, and all on board thought she would be pulled in pieces.

Haley called Aleck Bell and asked him to organize in one compact body, make a sudden assault on the roughs and drive forward into the steerage and place them under guard, but in no case was a revolver to be fired, unless in absolute self-defense. "Hit them over the heads," said Haley, "but don't shoot; I desire this to be a bloodless victory." Still the successful transfer of passengers went bravely on. Soon the armed Goliah's passengers, under Aleck Bell, quietly (all who were not seasick), by a successful maneuver, took possession of the after end of the cabin and Aleck gave the order, "All of the men in this cabin will go forward to the steerage; the cabin is to be exclusively devoted to the ladies and children." No one moved. "Charge 'em, boys," said Aleck, at the same time belting a rough bully on the head with his revolver, and "at 'em" it was.

The onset was so sudden, so unexpected, so different from what they looked for, that they at once gave way, and like sheep were driven into the steerage, where John McMullen, with a picked guard, kept them until Captain Burt and Charley Mathews, both passengers, in command of boats, were ready to commence removing the rapidly accumulating living cargo to the providentially found landing place. Then the roughs were marched out of the steerage in detachments through files armed with revolvers, placed in the Goliah's boats and sent on shore.

"All day the transfer of passengers went on, without an accident; all day the gallant Goliah groaned, labored and creaked, with waves sometimes breaking over her bows and washing her decks. Still no accident had occurred, and at sunset the last soul on board the wreck had been safely transferred to the Goliah, nearly half of whom had been retransferred to the land, with water and provisions enough landed with them to do them for a day or two, and this brilliant nautical feat was a splendid success. But none too soon, for by this time the wind had commenced to blow, and by dark had become a gale, and by the time the Goliah was well clear of her dangerous neighbor, and before dark obscured our vision the gallant Yankee Blade, with her golden treasure, broke in two amidships, and sank in deep water. The gallant Goliah, with her happy crew, brave commander, and thankful passengers, after a rough night of it, reached Santa Barbara, discharged a part of her human freight, and thence to San Pedro, where more were put on shore, while the remainder we taken back to San Diego and left, and the staunch old steamer hurried back, and took on board all that had been landed on the beach at the place of the wreck, and carried them in safety to San Francisco, all without a single casualty; and save some forty or fifty lives that were lost in the swamping of the boats of the Yankee Blade before the Goliah arrived, all of that hive of human beings were carried back in safety to San Francisco. Will the reader now agree with the author that the gallant Captain Haley was entitled to a reward of honor equal to any ever conferred by ancient Rome or modern France? And had he been an Englishman, the Cross of Victoria, at least, would have been conferred on him, to be treasured up as a reminder to his descendants of the noble deed of their ancestor.

There were many heroes on that dark and wind-swept night many years ago, but also many scalawags. The greatest hero of all was Captain Haley of the GOLIAH. Not many ship captains sailing the seven seas those days would have been willing to put their vessel, cargo, and passengers at risk in the surf-line of an unfriendly shore. Captain Haley was most innovative in the method he used to drop his anchors, and then back his ship down to the wreck. He floated a line aboard the YANKEE BLADE and then, using his "steam-power," cinched up on his anchors. A lifeboat was ringed to the taut line while another line was used to pull the lifeboat back and forth between the BLADE and the GOLIAH. This rescue of all passengers that had been left aboard the YANKEE BLADE was accomplished without incident or loss of life. It was truly the work of a genius and it couldn't have been done without the recent invention of steam propulsion. Captain Haley was not only the master of his ship, but also a master of the sea.

Today for those seeking the sunken treasure of the YANKEE BLADE at the graveyard of ships off of Point Pedernales, there may be a problem. There were nine crates of "specie," consisting of coin, gold dust, and bar gold in the "official" ship's cargo. All nine boxes were recovered in the months following this disaster. The passenger losses of gold and valuables would be worth $500,000 at today's price, and very little of this has ever been found. It could be spread over a vast area of sea floor, covered by years of silt and sand. The big problem for today's treasure hunter is the fact that also buried on the seafloor are naval shells and ammunition from the destroyer catastrophe of 1923. Adding to this problem is the fact that this is a highly restricted area belonging to the Vandenburg Air Force Base Missile Range!

The "boys in Air Force blue" would frown on those snooping around looking for golden trinkets.

Which city is furthest east of San Francisco: Los Angeles, Seattle, Honolulu, Reno, or San Diego?

Most people will say Reno; a few say Honolulu because they are confused about east and west; but if you said San Diego, you are correct! Don't take our word...look at a map.

Here is another question for you. The country of Chile in South America is directly south of Los Angeles, San Antonio, or New York?

—Chapter Twenty-One—

EL PRESIDENTE WAS A GRINGO

Near the equator the hot, humid tropical air becomes stifling. The humidity in Nicaragua is similar to southern Florida during the summer months. The day swelters and the dank, sultry atmosphere makes a person sweaty, sticky, and most uncomfortable. And that's wearing Bermuda shorts and a tank top!

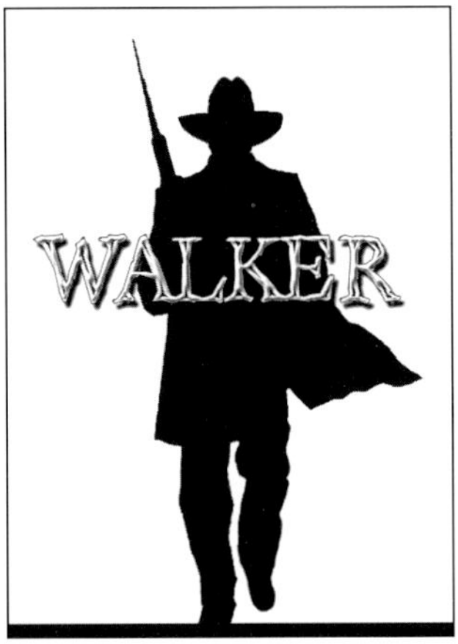

What would it be like in an all black business suit with vest, including gold watch and chain, black cloak, and a black preacher hat? William Walker wore just that style of dress when he brought an army of men from California to invade Nicaragua and almost changed the world.

William Walker, medical doctor, lawyer, writer, and soldier of fortune, was born in Nashville, Tennessee, May 8, 1824. He became President of Nicaragua in 1856 at the age of thirty-two and was executed at the hands of a Honduran firing squad in 1860 at the age of thirty-six. At the time his name was well known throughout the world; however the name of Walker did not survive, so today very few people, including historians, know of Walker's exploits.

Who was this "gringo" that led an army to Central America? What were his objectives, and how was he financed? How was the United States of America embarrassed by his military endeavors? How did the American Civil War and the building of the Panama Canal defeat Walker's objectives after his death?

William Walker was only five feet five and weighed 120 pounds. Often mocked by his peers as being "short, slight, towheaded, freckle-faced, shy, bookish, and oversensitive," Walker was described as having a long straight nose, a wide mouth, an unwrinkled brow beneath light brown hair, an angular jaw, and heavy-lidded eyes.

It was his eyes that gave him his power. Grey, brilliant, luminous eyes, that seemed to penetrate the skulls of the men he talked to. They quickened the interest of friends, arrested strangers, and threw antagonists off balance. He would become known throughout the world as "the grey-eyed man."

William Walker was an exceptional student, having entered the University of Nashville at age twelve, majoring in theological studies, and graduating at the young age of fourteen. Upon his graduation, Walker attended the medical college at the University of Pennsylvania, graduating in 1843 at age nineteen. His medical studies continued in France at the Sorbonne.

Disillusionment with the medical profession dictated that he return home, but not before he toured important sites of the old continent where he quickly learned to speak French, German, and Spanish. Relocating from Nashville to New Orleans, he positioned himself to study law. At age twenty-three Walker passed the bar exam and became qualified to practice law. However, before becoming a "legal eagle" he was approached by the owners of a newly formed conservative newspaper to become the news editor, writing on issues of foreign affairs.

During this time, Walker had met and fallen in love with Ellen Galt Martin whom he planned to marry in the very near future. Her untimely death from cholera and the financial failure of the newspaper caused Walker to decide to begin a new life in San Francisco. The next few months of Walker's life are a closed book as there is no record of his travels to California. As a newspaper editor, he was quite familiar with the hardships suffered by those crossing the Sierra Nevada, as well as the difficulties encountered crossing the Isthmus of Panama. He probably did not make the long voyage by sea around South America either.

It was the opinion of many that Walker had taken a steamer from New Orleans to Nicaragua, crossed over the narrow land mass to the Pacific Ocean, and caught a ship to San Francisco. What we do know is that Walker showed up in downtown San Francisco with a deep, weather-beaten tan, dusty clothes, a broad-brimmed black hat, and was almost penniless.

The new state of California had recently been admitted to the Union and Walker was again attracted to the newspaper business. He became one of the editors of the *Daily Herald* and as an advocate of anti-crime crusades he became an instant celebrity.

His success in challenging the California courts could have led to a very successful career in politics, however he declined to go that route, by transporting people and materials to the gold fields of California.

Walker was known throughout the world for his exploits in Nicaragua, but he actually began his escapades in Mexico. In fact, Walker and his law partner, Henry P. Watkins, from Marysville, California, were directly involved with the failed attempt to take over Baja, California, and the aborted invasion of Sonora, Mexico.

The next two chapters examine the details of Walker's military escapades and how he briefly became the "gringo" president of the Central American nation of Nicaragua and how he "offended" the Commodore.

—Chapter Twenty-two—

THE MEXICAN EXPEDITION

The Treaty of Guadalupe Hidalgo, which was signed by both Mexico and the United States at the end of the Mexican War, had two major defects in the establishment of border boundaries. The first mistake was its failure to allow for a seaport for American access to the Gulf of California. Walker and his backers felt that territory allowing this access could easily be secured from the defeated nation of Mexico by introducing a force of Americans into Sonora under the guise of colonists. This sleight-of-hand would save Walker and his colonists from being accused of violating the neutrality laws. There were rumors that powers within the American federal government supported Walker financially in raising an army of men for the invasion of the area.

Fred Collins cachet #O2313

The second mistake in the treaty was regarding the requirement that the United States police the Indians in the territory north of the newly established border. The Mexican Army was unable to stop raids by the Apache and Comanche Indians against the small Mexican villages or pueblos south of the border. There were an estimated 160,000 Indians south of the Gila River, which constituted the border of the New Mexico Territory. The United States stationed more than 8,000 troops along this border to keep the peace; however, the military expenditures between 1848 and 1853 were astronomical, and the Indian raids still continued into Mexico. Walker and his group felt that by colonizing Sonora, the Mexican population would welcome Walker and his men with open arms, because they would help stop the raids. It is interesting to note that Walker's backers were wealthy California gold mine owners, and that Sonora, Mexico, had many gold mines. Again, the powers in Washington were rumored to have looked the other way as Walker recruited his troops.

In San Francisco, between the end of the war in 1848 and statehood in 1850, there was a huge population influx due mainly to the discovery of gold. At one time during this period, 500 abandoned ships lay rotting in the tide land of San Francisco Bay. The crews had deserted and headed for Sacramento to make their fortune. Many of these people became disenchanted because they did not find gold, or because they became victims of others who robbed them of their wealth. Wagon trains continued to pour over the mountains or across the deserts. There were very few laws, and even fewer people to back up what law and order did exist. Vigilante groups were formed and many hangings took place. Roughnecks, murderers, drunks, and outlaws roamed city streets. It was not difficult for Walker and his recruiters to sign up these so-called adventurers, including sailors to sail the ships. Walker easily put together a rag-tag army, then sailed with the morning tide on October 8, 1853 for Guaymas, Mexico, the main seaport of Sonora.

Walker learned that a strong Mexican army unit was garrisoned at Guaymas, and he felt that he should wait until his partner, Henry Watkins, set sail from San Francisco with supplies and additional recruits. The decision was made that his first conquest would be the sparsely populated peninsula of Baja California, just across the Sea of Cortez (Gulf of California) from Sonora. The capital city of the Baja is La Paz, where Walker landed his force. Without a shot being fired, the troops quickly captured the governor and hauled down the Mexican flag, replacing it with the flag of the "Republic of Lower California."

Walker proclaimed to the people of La Paz that they were free from the tyranny of Mexico, and that all the inhabitants of Lower California no longer owed allegiance to Mexico. He would act as president of the Republic until it became a firmly established new nation.

A small Mexican force from Guaymas made a landing in La Paz but were beaten back by Walker's men. It was learned that a larger force was to sail from Guaymas to La Paz the next day so Walker decided again to wait for his supply ships and reinforcements. Since Walker's ultimate objective was Sonora, he decided not to take on the Mexican Army coming from Guaymas, but rather take a northern route, crossing into mainland

Baja California and Mexico's West Coast

Mexico from the Baja by land just south of the U.S./Mexican border. Sailing northward along the Pacific Coast of the Baja, Walker and his army landed at Ensenada, which is one hundred miles south of the American border. Again without bloodshed, the town was taken, a proclamation read, and the "Republic of Lower California" flag was hoisted for all to see.

The first order of business for Walker was to make a list of "cabinet appointments" of Americans, consisting mainly of the rogues in his army. This list was sent to San Francisco, along with a statement for the newspapers. The statement declared that Lower California had been shamefully neglected by the Mexican government, and that it had been necessary for a new republic to be created in order to develop the resources of the peninsula, and effect a proper social organization therein.

Two hundred Mexican soldiers stationed at what today would be Tijuana, marched south to Ensenada and gave battle to Walker's troops. After three days of bloody fighting, the attackers were routed. The day after the battle, Walker was astounded to see his ship hoist anchor, and put to sea, headed southward towards La Paz. What the "gray-eyed gringo" hadn't counted on, had happened! The governor of La Paz, when captured, had been put in chains aboard Walker's ship. Being a super salesman, the governor had convinced the ship's officers that great wealth awaited them if he was returned to La Paz and that there was no future for the ship officers by continuing on with Walker and his illegal army. The biggest blow to Walker was the fact that the ship stored most of the food for his troops.

Two more setbacks faced Walker and they would ultimately spell defeat to his endeavors. The first was the arrival by sea of his partner, Watkins, with 230 armed men and enough guns and ammunition to take on the entire Mexican army. But there was no food aboard the ship, so now Walker was desperate for supplies. Watkins was immediately sent back to Alta California in search of more food. Meanwhile, Walker raided nearby ranches for beef and corn, and put all troops on half ration. His army, already weakened by diseases, resented the food shortage and Walker's strict measures of discipline. His standing orders were that any man found robbing a house or raping a woman would be shot. It was okay to run off livestock from the local ranches but another thing to enter the house and rob the occupants.

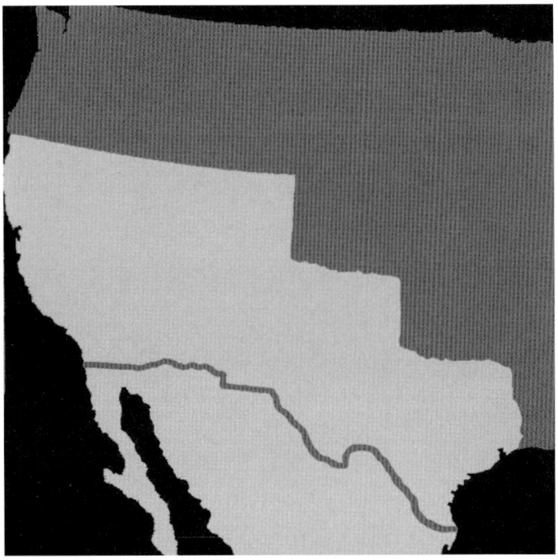

Land obtained from Mexico by the Treaty of Guadalupe Hidalgo.

The second setback was Walker's death knell. Our history books call it the Gadsden Purchase. It seems that when the Treaty of Guadalupe Hidalgo was signed at the end of the war, a map maker by the name of Disturnell, used a reprint of an 1828 map of Mexico, which in turn was a reproduction of an 1822 map. These maps were grossly in error because they placed the Rio Grande too far west and the town of El Paso too far south of their true locations. The rich Mesilla Valley, along with its mining district, would remain in Mexico. This was not acceptable to the United States. In addition, by using the Gila River as the boundary-line, the problem of Indian raids into Mexico was aggravated. James Gadsden, representing the United States, was sent to Mexico to negotiate a treaty to purchase the northern portion of Sonora for ten million dollars. The Mexican government felt this price was extremely low, but they also feared that the American government secretly controlled the raids by

Walker, and if the purchase offer was refused, they stood a chance of losing both the Baja peninsula and Sonora without receiving any compensation. The Mexicans were right, of course, as many Americans felt that occupation of all of Mexico should have been the prize for the U.S. victory. When the provisional treaty was signed on December 31, 1853, Gadsden issued a separate letter assuring the Mexican government that the United States regarded Walker as a violator of federal law and that he would be dealt with accordingly. Once the New Mexico territory was in American hands, Walker's expedition into Sonora lost its appeal and the barren real estate of the Baja was not a high priority for the American public.

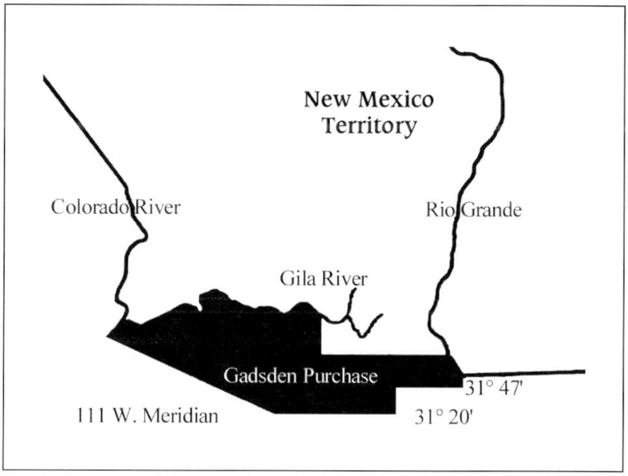

The Gadsden Purchase, 1853.

Meanwhile, Walker continued to have problems. A Mexican gunboat patrolled the entrance to Ensenada, stopping all shipment of supplies and additional manpower to his army. When word was received of the Gadsden Purchase, Walker realized his only option was to march overland to Sonora. The troops agreed to fight rather than go through the humiliation of surrender.

The overland trek began with 130 men. It was fortunate that this desert region was not tackled during the summer months. When they arrived in Sonora, Walker's soldiers were in rags and their boots were worn through. Without food or hope, the men were completely finished. No one had welcomed them with open arms as Walker had earlier anticipated. The soldiers retraced their steps, down the mountain trails, across the desert, and on May 8, 1854 (which incidentally was Walker's thirtieth birthday) they entered San Diego and surrendered to the military authorities. It is worth noting that Walker did not surrender as President of Lower California, but in his words, "I am Colonel

William Walker; I wish to surrender my force to the United States." He was arraigned before the federal court in San Francisco on an indictment by the grand jury, and charged with violation of the neutrality laws.

Walker's real claim to fame and his defeat in Nicaraguan campaigns will be explored in the next chapter.

—Chapter Twenty-three—

THE NICARAGUAN EXPEDITION

What was America's (and therefore William Walker's) interest in Nicaragua in the middle of the nineteenth century? Many engineers and politicians of the time considered Nicaragua to be "the best place for an effective waterway passage from one ocean to the other." Many people still feel the same way.

During the California gold rush, Cornelius Vanderbilt constructed a railway across Nicaragua that allowed prospectors and other immigrants to sail from New York to San Juan del Norte, ride by train across southern Nicaragua to San Juan del Sur, and there board another Vanderbilt steamer bound for San Francisco. When William Walker invaded the country and became "El Presidente" (more on that later), he seized the charter of Vanderbilt's Accessory Transit Company, in one fell swoop making Vanderbilt his sworn enemy and initiating interest in the Isthmus of Panama as the "second best" route for Atlantic/Pacific passage.

What about a canal in Nicaragua? It is the largest republic in Central America, and also the poorest. The tiny population amounts to 4.5 million people, most of whom live in a 100 kilometer-wide strip along the Pacific Coast. There are very few cities on the Caribbean side.

The key to a "wet" canal crossing Nicaragua is the large Lago de Nicaragua (lago means lake) which could be called the ninth wonder of the world. The lake is ninety-two miles long and about thirty-four miles in width. Thousands of years ago this large saltwater bay was part of the Pacific

The Panama Canal was started by the French in 1881 and continued to 1889, when it was taken over by United States companies, and finished in 1914. It was a very costly operation, not only in money, but primarily in lives lost to disease and accident. A quote from the French government printed in a local paper said, "If you try to build this canal, there will not be trees enough on the isthmus to make crosses for the graves of your laborers." The total lives lost by the French and American companies were 27,798 or more than 500 deaths for each mile of the canal's fifty-five mile length. The distance from New York to San Francisco is 13,515 miles by way of Cape Magellan (around the The Horn) and only 6,080 miles using the Panama Canal. The distance saved is 7,873 miles or four lives lost for each mile saved!

From 1914 to the end of World War II in 1945, the canal was a strategic military asset as well as a time and cost saving transit for international commercial shipping. Then the maritime nations of the world decided to build larger ships to haul cargo more efficiently. The canal can only handle ships up to 965 feet in length, 106 feet maximum width (beam) and a gross weight (displacement) of not more than 96,000 tons. Today's nuclear aircraft carriers are 257 feet wide, and the giant oil tankers are 250,000 tons and better. The Panama Canal is restricted to ships with a maximum size similar to the Love Boat, or smaller.

Ocean. Earthquakes closed off the body of water, trapping the ocean creatures. As rivers flowed into the lake the salt water was gradually replaced with fresh water. Today, this is the only spot in the world where sharks, lobsters, and other saltwater creatures can be found in fresh water.

The landmass that seals off this geological lake, that was once open to the Pacific, is only fifteen miles wide. The Rio San Juan, at the southern tip of the lake at San Carlos, runs eastward mostly along the border of Costa Rica, and empties into the Caribbean. What is amazing is the fact that all rivers in the area begin in mountainous regions of Nicaragua and flow downward into the lake—but not the San Juan—it starts and ends at sea level. This means that no series of locks would be required such as

Modern aircraft carrier, too large to traverse the Panama Canal

those required in the Panama Canal. It would be simply a matter of digging a sea level canal from the lake to the Pacific Ocean port of Juan del Sur (see map). This natural sea level route could then be used for even the largest ocean going vessels if the San Juan River were widened and straightened.

There are several large islands in the Lago de Nicaragua. These are old and dormant volcanoes that had important influence on the decision by the United States to finish the Panama Canal. In 1900, at the turn of the twentieth century, Nicaragua had issued a postal stamp with a picture of the lake and islands. In order to be historically accurate, the stamp artist drew a wisp of smoke coming from the conical volcano. A Panamanian lobbyist, representing the case for a Panama Canal

Cruise ship typical of ships still using canal.

The United States built the Panama Canal but did not own it—it was leased from the government of Panama—or at least it was for eighty-six years! The original lease was signed for a period of time "in perpetuity" which gave us the right of management of the canal corridor known as the Canal Zone. In the years after World War II the United States realized the obsolescence of the canal and President Jimmy Carter signed a bill relinquishing the U.S. holdings effective on January 1, 2000. The only right we retained was of "first priority passage in time of war." This arrangement between sovereign nations (Panama and the U.S.) is okay in concept, but might be deficient in reality.

On December 31, 1999 the United States vacated the Canal Zone and turned all facilities, including military bases, over to the Panama Ports Company. The Panama Ports Company is a subsidiary of Hutchison Whampoa Ltd., which is a Hong Kong based company whose chairman reportedly has close ties to the Chinese Communist People's Liberation Army! And on July 1, 1997, Hong Kong reverted to being a province of the People's Republic of China.

The Clinton Administration was silent on this matter, however retired Admiral Thomas Moorer, former Joint Chiefs of Staff Chairman, had this to say, "I don't see how any reasonably intelligent person can fail to see the vital strategic importance of the canal. The Chinese see it, obviously."

to the United States Senate, used these stamps to his advantage. Everyone in Washington, D.C. received a stamp, including the members of the Senate, with a note from the lobbyist asking, "What happens to the Nicaraguan Transit Route the next time the volcano erupts?" This scare campaign worked, and the decision to go ahead with the Panama project was approved—even though it wasn't the best waterway route.

Today, talks are underway to consider a "dry" canal in Nicaragua, as the expense for a "wet" canal and its environmental impact may not make it viable. With military readiness being more dependent on pre-positioned naval task forces and quick response aircraft units, perhaps the "wet" canal approach is obsolete in today's military strategies. The "land-bridge" or "dry canal" concept would be created by the construction of deep-water container ports and free-trade zones on the Pacific and Caribbean sides of Nicaragua—connected by a 210-mile high-speed railway. Container ships would off-load cargo onto flatbed railway cars, and then, a few hours later, the containers would be loaded onto a waiting ship at the other end.

Maybe the Panama Canal, with its worn-out equipment and size restrictions, is also obsolete. Maybe the Chinese have bought a pig-in-a-poke. If the Chinese raise transit rates in the future, or deny passage to love boat types of cruise ships and passengers, the ships could go around the "Horn" without much difficulty, just as they did in the 1850s and the "dry" canal in Nicaragua would become very financially attractive.

What was the story of William Walker and his role in Nicaragua? Walker could have been a very wealthy practicing attorney, landowner, and politician if he had put his roots down in California. Being a proud man consumed with the idea of a "manifest destiny" both for America and himself, he became known as a filibuster. In today's world we think of a filibuster as a delaying tactic used primarily in the United States Senate. In Walker's day, a filibuster was mainly known, for lack of a kinder word, as a pirate. It meant the dominance of the weak by the strong. The thought most prominent in Walker's mind and in the minds of others like him, was that if the regions (California and Central America) did not become a part of the United States, some other nation, stronger than Mexico, would grasp them.

The United States government, of course, could not officially condone such practice even within the Monroe Doctrine; however, it could look the other way, or even wink at Walker's filibustering ways. Had Walker been successful in the Sonora expedition, probably half of San Francisco would have joined him and both the Baja and Sonora would have become a part of the United States.

The fiasco in Baja California was not what Walker was best known for—it was his later exploits in Central America that earned him his place in history. Having been arrested in violation of the neutrality laws, Walker was tried in the federal courts at San Francisco but acquitted!

At that time in Nicaragua there was a war between two factions: the Granada faction was at war with the Leonese. The Leonese were on the verge of being defeated and desperately sought the aid of Walker and whatever army he could put together and bring to the battlefield.

San Francisco during the 1850s was rough and tough, with many disenchanted miners who had been unsuccessful in the gold fields, as well as sailors who had jumped ship and others of a questionable background. The recruitment of followers as soldiers of fortune was not a difficult task for Walker. Ships were plentiful, hundreds having been abandoned in the bay by their crews.

As an example of the United States government looking the other way, Walker was ready to set sail on May 3, 1855, when the U.S. Marshall tried to stop his departure. Walker contacted General Wool, the military commander on the Pacific coast, and when told of Walker's plans, the general not only officially ignored the project, but also privately shook hands and wished Walker success.

Walker actually made three expeditions to Nicaragua. The first made him a hero, the next two led to his downfall and death.

Upon landing in Nicaragua and contacting the Leonese, Walker and his army marched on the town of Rivas. For his victory there, he was given the title of Generalissimo. The people of Nicaragua loved him as a savior, and when he achieved additional military victories, he was declared President of Nicaragua. Viva La Nicaragua! Viva El Presidente! Viva El Gringo!

When news reached the United States, money was raised and many more soldiers of fortune went south to aid Walker in his military sojourns. With all this new power now in Walker's hands, he started to manage things his way. He realized that in controlling Nicaragua, he would also be the sole controller of the transit route. His first order of business was to revoke the franchise held by Cornelius Vanderbilt and hand the reigns over to his old buddy and former law partner from New Orleans, Edmond

Randolf. This was a huge mistake. Vanderbilt had but one philosophy, and that was, "Don't get mad, get even!" And he did just that! The Commodore, as Cornelius was known, lived by a famous quote by Sir Walter Raleigh that hung on his office wall: "Whoever commands the sea, commands the trade, whoever commands the trade of the world, commands the riches of the world, and consequently the world itself."

Walker's second mistake was the issuing of a proclamation reversing the anti-slavery laws that had existed for thirty-two years in Nicaragua. This caused great concern within the native population and led to revolts throughout the nation.

Commodore Vanderbilt then effectively cut off all supply lines to Walker's army, and being closely tied to the government of Costa Rica, the Commodore convinced that nation to attack Nicaragua. Walker had been in command less than two years when he was forced to leave the country.

In November, 1857, Walker had formed a new army and landed at Punta Arenas, but this expedition, too, was to be short-lived. He immediately declared himself commander of the Nicaraguan army. Commodore Pauling of the United States Caribbean Squadron landed a force of Marines and demanded Walker's surrender. He was brought back to the United States where President Buchanan condemned Walker as a filibuster. Walker was tried for violation of the neutrality law, but again, the case was dismissed.

Walker's next military adventure was to land his army near Truxillo, Honduras, where he planned to travel overland and invade Nicaragua from the north. His men began to desert him and Walker was finally forced to surrender to the captain of a British naval vessel. The captain had promised Walker safe passage to the United States where he would be turned over to the authorities. Instead of keeping his word, the British captain handed Walker over to the Honduran authorities. The court martial trial only took a few short hours. Found guilty, Walker was marched out and placed in front of a brick wall where the firing squad did their duty. The date was September 12, 1860. Justice comes swift in Latin American countries!

NO MÁS EL GRINGO! EL PRESIDENTE IS DEAD!

AUTHOR'S EPILOGUE

In closing, I would like to point out that in writing this book about little known "happenings" in California's early history, I did not intend to ignore the many stories about the gold rush and the colorful towns and people involved. Many books have been written about the gold fields but I chose to overlook these mining town stories in order to bring you, the reader, the facts on how California was discovered, explored, and settled.

The time span of this book from exploration in 1769 to the death of William Walker in 1860 is only ninety-one years. However, these years were critical in the birth, adolescence, and adulthood of our truly fine utopia known as California. Some may not find or choose to call California a utopia, but it is as close to being one as any place that I know of. I say that not only because I am a native son, born and raised here, but also because I have lived a number of years in Oregon and New Mexico. I've also spent many enjoyable months in Arizona and Nevada and internationally in the Orient, Australia, Mexico, and Canada. California is truly unique in this world.

This book brought many hours of enjoyment doing the research, just as I hope it brought you the same in reading it. I am reminded, when traveling in California's great "outback" described in the first chapter, "In the Beginning There Was Nothing." There is still a lot of "nothing" out there when crossing our great deserts and mountain ranges.

I was amazed at the hardships of terrain, weather, and supply problems facing the Spanish as they built their "ladder of missions." And how about that pirate, "Old Hippo," who sacked our capital of Monterey. I had always thought pirates were only in other parts of the world, such as the Caribbean.

My research for the Mexican Period led me from San Salvador Island (Catalina) to the Fort Ross of the Russians, and then on to Sutter's Fort. My favorite chapter is "Land-Water-Sun," about the Carillo family and the romance and marriage of the young Spanish señoritas to the American ship captains.

The chapters about Thomas Larkin and the lowering of the Mexican flag at Monterey four years before war was declared, and the escapades of Lieutenant Archibald Gillespie, U.S.M.C. were truly fun to research. John

Fremont with his "dumb little cannon" that he hauled all over creation was exciting to learn about. Perhaps some readers of this book will locate the "lost cannon" someday and write their version of the challenge.

The chapter about Pre-Marshall Gold was a real eye-opener. It reminded me of the old cliché, "Golden Rule—he who owns the gold, rules!"

General Kearny and his army truly brought home the facts of how the west was won. I live in Escondido, only a few miles from Mule Hill and the battle site. I often think of this military encounter that transpired only a few short years ago, across the glen from my home.

The last chapter in the Mexican Period, War in the Baja, made me appreciate the politics that went on involving Mexico retaining ownership of this very fine real estate. In fact, the loss of the Baja led to the chapters in the American Period about the exploits of William Walker in the Baja as well as Central America.

James King of William really caught my attention! I never realized as I walked through the streets of San Francisco a number of years ago (my office was at the corner of Montgomery and California Streets) what colorful history had taken place all around me.

Very few Californians know about the Graveyard of Ships and of the many people who lost their lives on our treacherous coastline. This chapter was exciting, especially learning about the steamboat races. One normally thinks of paddle-wheelers racing each other up and down the Mississippi River, but not out on the Pacific Ocean.

We discussed in Chapter Eighteen some minorities in early California. They still exist today. Within the cities, as well as many small towns, there are entire communities of minorities stemming from Asian, Latin, and Black roots. On the whole, the entire population of the state seems to function well with little conflict.

For those living in California, and for those that may visit in the future, let me say in closing, "Enjoy and God Bless."

Insignias of California

ANIMAL

The grizzly bear was officially designated State Animal in 1953. Seventy-five years after discovery of gold, the last grizzly in California had been tracked down and killed. The grizzly roamed the great valleys and low mountain areas of California much like the great herds of buffalo on the American plains. Unlike the buffalo or deer, grizzly bears traveled in a "troop" rather than a herd. They killed livestock and disrupted settler's crops. As California became more populated, the grizzly finally became extinct within the state, however they still can be found in other areas of the west.

BIRD

In 1931, the California quail known as the Valley Quail, became the official state bird. Smaller than a pigeon, this plump gray-colored bird with black plume on top of its head and black bib with white stripe under the beak, travels in pairs during the spring. The pair nest in hollows scratched in the ground, concealed by heavy brush, where five to twenty-five creamy white eggs are laid. The eggshells are well camouflaged with speckles of golden brown.

COLORS

The official colors of California which were passed by the State Legislature in 1951 are a combination of blue and gold. The blue represents the clear sky (which is more often than not), and the gold is the color of precious metal found by the forty-niners. The University of California, Berkeley, first used these colors in 1875.

FISH

An act of the State Legislature in 1947 named the Golden Trout as the official state fish. This native to California only, was first found in the headwaters south of Mount Whitney, the highest peak in the continental United States. Today, both wild and hatchery-reared golden trout are found in most high elevations of the Sierra Nevada mountains, as well as being planted in other states.

FLAG

As we read in an earlier chapter, a small band of settlers marched on June 14, 1846 against the Mexican garrison at Sonoma. This uprising became known as the Bear Flag Revolt. The handmade flag, replacing the Mexican flag, consisted of a grizzly bear and a five-pointed star over a red bar and the words "California Republic." As we went to war with Mexico, the bear flag was soon replaced with the stars and stripes of the American flag. The California State Legislature adopted the Bear Flag in 1911 as the official state flag.

FLOWER

The Golden Poppy, which grows wild throughout California, became the state flower in 1903. Each year, on April 6, Californians honor the flower on California Poppy Day.

FOSSIL

The Sabre-Tooth Cat was adopted by the Legislature in 1973 as the official State Fossil. This tiger-sized cat roamed throughout California forty million years ago as evidenced by the fossil bones found in well preserved abundance at the La Brea Tar Pits of Los Angeles.

GEMSTONE

An extremely rare gemstone, named Benitoite, was designated the official California Gemstone in 1985. It was first discovered near the headwaters of the San Benito River from which it derives its name. Referred to as the "blue diamond," it ranges in color from a shade of violet to a light transparent blue, and sometimes to a dark vivid sapphire blue.

INSECT

The Doghead Butterfly, sometimes called the California Dogface, became the official State Insect in 1972. It is usually found in the foothills of the Sierra Nevada mountains, but also can be found in the coastal ranges between Sonoma and San Diego. The female butterfly is entirely yellow with a black spot on the upper wings, while the male has a distinctive yellow silhouette of a dog's head on its wings.

MARINE FISH

The State Legislature named the Garibaldi as official State Marine Fish in 1995. Although the garibaldi is not on the endangered species list, there is a moratorium on commercial collection until the year 2002. The reason for this is the popularity of the garibaldi by the saltwater aquarium collectors. The garibaldi can be found in shallow waters off the Southern California coast. It is approximately fourteen inches in length with a golden orange coloring. The baby garibaldi are even more colorful with bright blue spots on a reddish orange body.

MARINE MAMMAL

The California Gray Whale, designated the State Marine Mammal in 1975, measures thirty-five to fifty feet in length and weighs in at twenty to forty tons. These "little guys" spend their summers in the Bering Sea then travel southward 7,000 miles during December through February to the bays and lagoons of Baja, California, returning to Alaska in March and April. The migration follows the California coastline and tourists by the hundreds cram into small boats for the spectator sport of whale watching.

MINERAL

As you can probably guess, Gold is the official State Mineral and was so designated in 1965. Between 1850 and 1859, over ten billion dollars' worth of gold was mined from California, and even today, prospectors can still pan for the yellow metal in California streams.

MOTTO

The Greek word "Eureka," which means "I have found it," appears in the Great Seal of California as explained on the cover page. Attempts were made in 1957 to use "In God We Trust" as the state motto, but Eureka was made official in 1963. The Greek mathematician, Archimedes, is said to have used the word when he discovered a method to determine the purity of gold.

NICKNAME

"The Golden State" became official in 1968, describing the scenic beauty of the golden poppy fields that can be seen every spring throughout the state. Of course, the discovery of gold in 1848 added to the nickname.

PREHISTORIC ARTIFACT

California is the first state to designate an official prehistoric artifact. This archaeological treasure is believed to have been carved by California's earliest inhabitants some 8,000 years ago and was found in a dig site in San Diego County. The chipped stone symbol in volcanic rock, resembling a walking bear, is only two and a half inches by one and a half inches.

REPTILE

Some of you may speculate that the rattlesnake would be the State Reptile, however, the race was won for the designation in 1972 by the speedster known as a Desert Tortoise. This tortoise can travel about twenty feet per minute, which translates to a full football field in about an hour! This desert vegetarian has existed on earth for millions of years and now enjoys its protected status as an endangered species.

ROCK

California was also the first state to designate a State Rock. Serpentine is a shiny green and blue rock found throughout California, and is composed of chromite, magnesite, and cinnabar. California also has the distinction of having a wider variety and greater number of minerals than any other state.

SEAL

The Great Seal of California has already been discussed on the page regarding the cover of this book.

SONG

I Love You California was written by Los Angeles businessman, F. B. Silverwood—the words appear on the next page.

TREE

In 1937 the State Legislature designated the California Redwood as the official tree. There are actually two species of California redwood: the Coast Redwood and the Giant Sequoia. The General Sherman Tree in

Sequoia National Park is 272 feet high and more than thirty-six feet in diameter. It is considered to be the world's largest tree overall. The tallest redwoods can be found in the Humboldt area of the coastal range. One monster tree reaches skyward 360 feet.

I LOVE YOU, CALIFORNIA

BY F. B. Silverwood

I.

I love you, California, you're the greatest state of all.
I love you in the winter, summer, spring, and in the fall.
I love your fertile valleys; your dear mountains I adore.
I love your grand old ocean and I love her rugged shore.

Chorus

Where the snow crowned Golden Sierras
Keep their watch o'er the valleys bloom,
It is there I would be in our land by the sea,
Every breeze bearing rich perfume.
It is here nature gives of her rarest. It is Home Sweet Home to me,
And I know when I die I shall breathe my last sigh
For my sunny California.

II.

I love your redwood forests—love your fields of yellow grain.
I love your summer breezes and I love your winter rain.
I love you, land of flowers; land of honey, fruit, and wine.
I love you, California; you have won this heart of mine.

III.

I love your old gray Missions—love your vineyards stretching far.
I love you, California, with your Golden Gate ajar.
I love your purple sunsets, love your skies of azure blue.
I love you, California; I just can't help loving you.

IV.

I love you, Catalina, you are very dear to me.
I love you, Tamalpais, and I love Yosemite.
I love you, Land of Sunshine, half your beauties are untold.
I loved you in my childhood, and I'll love you when I'm old.

CONSTITUTION OF THE STATE OF CALIFORNIA
[1849*]

We, the people of California, grateful to Almighty God for our freedom, in order to secure its blessings, do establish this Constitution.

ARTICLE I.

Declaration of Rights.

Sec. 1. All men are by nature free and independent, and have certain inalienable rights, among which are those of enjoying and defending life and liberty, acquiring, possessing, and protecting property: and pursuing and obtaining safety and happiness.

Sec. 2. All political power is inherent in the people. Government is instituted for the protection, security, and benefit of the people; and they have the right to alter or reform the same, whenever the public good may require it.

Sec. 3. The right of trial by jury shall be secured to all, and remain inviolate forever; but a jury trial may be waved by the parties, in all civil cases, in the manner to be prescribed by law.

Sec. 4. The free exercise and enjoyment of religious profession and worship, without discrimination or preference, shall forever be allowed in this State: and no person shall be rendered incompetent to be a witness on account of his opinions on matters of religious belief; but the liberty of conscience, hereby secured, shall not be so construed as to excuse acts of licentiousness, or justify practices inconsistent with the peace or safety of this State.

Sec. 5. The privilege of the writ of habeas corpus shall not be suspended, unless when, in cases of rebellion or invasion, the public safety may require its suspension.

Sec. 6. Excessive bail shall not be required, nor excessive fines imposed, nor shall cruel or unusual punishments be inflicted, nor shall witnesses be unreasonably detained.

Sec. 7. All persons shall be bailable, by sufficient sureties: unless for capital offences, when the proof is evident or the presumption great.

Sec. 8. No person shall be held to answer for a capital or otherwise infamous crime, (except in cases of impeachment, and in cases of militia when in actual service, and the land naval forces in time of war, or which this State may keep with the consent of Congress in time of peace, and in cases of petit larceny under the regulation of the Legislature) unless on presentment or indictment of a grand jury; and in any trial in any court whatever, the party accused shall be allowed to appear and defend in person and with counsel, as in civil actions. No person shall be subject to be twice put jeopardy for the same offence; nor shall he be compelled, in any criminal case, to be a witness against himself, nor be deprived of life, liberty, or property, without due process of law; nor shall private property be taken for public use without just compensation.

Sec. 9. Every citizen may freely speak, write, and publish his sentiments on all subjects, being responsible for the abuse of that right; and no law shall be passed to restrain or abridge the liberty of speech or of the press. In all criminal prosecutions on indictments for libels, the truth may be given in evidence to the jury; and if it shall appear to the jury that the matter charged as libellous is true, and was published with good motives and for justifiable ends, the party shall be acquitted; and the jury shall have the right to determine the law and the fact.

Sec. 10. The people shall have the right freely to assemble together, to consult for the common good, to instruct their representatives, and to petition the legislature for redress of grievances.

Sec. 11. All laws of a general nature shall have a uniform operation.

Sec. 12. The military shall be subordinate to the civil power. No standing army shall be kept up by this State in time of peace; and in time of war no appropriation for a standing army shall be for a longer time than two years.

Sec. 13. No soldier shall, in time of peace, be quartered in any house, without the consent of the owner; nor in time of war, except in the manner to be prescribed by law.

Sec. 14. Representation shall be apportioned according to population.

Sec. 15. No person shall be imprisoned for debt, in any civil action on mesne or final process, unless in cases of fraud; and no person shall be imprisoned for a militia fine in time of peace.

Sec. 16. No bill of attainder, ex post facto law, or law impairing the obligation of contracts, shall ever be passed.

Sec. 17. Foreigners who are, of who may hereafter become bona fide residents if this State, shall enjoy the same rights in respect to the possession, enjoyment, and inheritance of property, as native born citizens,

Sec. 18. Neither slavery, nor involuntary servitude, unless for the punishment of crimes, shall ever be tolerated in this State.

Sec. 19. The right of the people to be secure in their persons, houses, papers and effects, against unreasonable seizures and searches, shall not be violated; and no warrant shall issue but on probable cause, supported by oath or affirmation, particularly describing the place to be searched, and the persons and things to be seized.

Sec. 20. Treason against the State shall consist only in levying war against it, adhering to its enemies, or giving them aid and comfort. No person shall be convicted of treason, unless the evidence of two witnesses to the same overt act, or confession in open court.

Sec. 21. This enumeration of rights shall not be construed to impair or deny others retained by the people.

ARTICLE II.

Right of Suffrage.

Sec. 1. Every white male citizen of the United States, and every white male citizen of Mexico, who shall have elected to become a citizen of the United States, under the treaty of peace exchanged and ratified at Queretaro, on the 30th day of May, 1848 of the age of twenty-one years, who shall have been a resident of the State six months next preceding the election, and the county or district in which he claims his vote thirty days, shall be entitled to vote at all elections which are now or hereafter may authorized by law: Provided, nothing herein contained, shall be construed to prevent the Legislature, by a two-thirds concurrent vote, from admitting to the right of suffrage, Indians or the descendants of Indians, in such special cases as such proportion of the legislative body may deem just and proper.

Sec. 2. Electors shall, in all cases except treason, felony, or breach of the peace, be privileged from arrest on the days of the election, during their attendance at such election, going to and returning therefrom.

Sec. 3. No elector shall be obliged to perform militia duty on the day of election, except in time of war or public danger.

Sec. 4. For the purpose of voting, no person shall be deemed to have gained or lost a residence by reason of his presence or absence while employed in the service of the United States; nor while engaged in the navigation of the waters of this State, or of the United States, or of the high seas; nor while a student of any seminary of learning; nor while kept at any almshouse, or other asylum, at public expense; nor while confined in any public prison.

Sec. 5. No idiot of insane person, or person convicted of any infamous crime, shall be entitled to the privilege of an elector.

Sec. 6. All elections by the people shall be by ballot.

ARTICLE III

Distribution of Powers

The powers of the Government of the State of California shall be divided into three separate departments: the Legislative, the Executive, and Judicial; and no person charged with the exercise of powers properly belonging to one of these departments, shall exercise any functions appertaining to either of the others, except in the cases hereinafter expressly directed or permitted.

ARTICLE IV

Legislative Department

Sec. 1. The Legislative power of this State shall be vested in a Senate and Assembly, which shall be designated the Legislature of the State of California; and enacting clause of every law shall be as follows: "The people of the State of California, represented in Senate and Assembly, do enact as follows."

Sec. 2. The sessions of the Legislature shall be annual, and shall commence on the first Monday of January, next ensuing the election of its members, unless the Governor of the State shall, in the interim, convene the Legislature by proclamaltion.

Sec. 3. The members of the Assembly shall be chosen annually, by the qualified electors of their respective districts, on the Tuesday next after the first Monday in November, unless otherwise ordered by the Legislature, and their term of office shall be one year.

Sec. 4. Senators and Members of Assembly shall be duly qualified electors in the respective counties and districts which they represent.

Sec. 5. Senators shall be chosen for the term of two years, at the same time and places as Members if Assembly; and no person shall be a member of the Senate or Assembly, who has not been a citizen and inhabitant of the State one year, and of the country or district for which he shall be chosen six months next before his election.

Sec. 6. The number of Senators shall not be less than one-third, nor more than one-half, of that of the Members of the Assembly; and at the first session of the Legislature after this Constitution takes effect, the Senators shall be divided by lot as equally as may be, into two classes; the seats of the Senators of the first class shall be vacated at the expiration of the first year, so that one-half shall be chosen annually.

Sec. 7. When the number of Senators is increased, they shall be apportioned by lot, so as to keep the two classes as nearly equal in number as possible.

Sec. 8. Each house shall choose its own officers and judge of the qualifications, elections, and returns of its own members.

Sec. 9. A majority of each house shall constitute a quorum to do business; but a smaller number may adjourn from day to day, and may compel the attendance of absent members, in such manner, and under such penalties, as each house may provide.

Sec. 10. Each house shall determine the rules of its own proceedings, and may, with the concurrence of two thirds of all members elected, expel a member.

Sec. 11. Each house shall keep a journal of its own proceedings, and publish the same; and the yeas and nays of the members of either house, on any question, shall at the desire of any three members present be entered on the journal.

Sec. 12. Members of the Legislature shall, in all cases except treason, felony, and breach of the peace, be privileged from arrest, and they shall not be subject to any civil process during the session of the Legislature, nor for fifteen days next before the commencement and after the termination of each session.

Sec. 13. When vacancies occur in either house, the Governor, or the person exercising the functions of the Governor, shall issue writs of election to fill such vacancies.

Sec. 14. The doors of each house shall be open, except on such occasions as, in the opinion of the House, may require secrecy.

Sec. 15. Neither house shall, without the consent of the other, adjourn for more than three days, nor to any other place than that in which they may be sitting.

Sec. 16. Any bill may originate in either house of the Legislature, and all bills passed by one house may be amended in the other.

Sec. 17. Every bill which may have passed the Legislature, shall, before it becomes a law, be presented to the Governor. If he approve it, he shall sign it; but if not, he shall return it, with his objections, to the house in which it originated, which shall enter the same upon the journal, and proceed to reconsider it. If, after such reconsideration, it again pass both houses, by yeas and nays, by a majority of two-thirds of the members of each house present, it shall become a law, notwithstanding the Governor's objections. If any bill shall not be returned within ten days after it shall have been presented to him, (Sunday excepted,) the same shall be a law, in like manner as if he had signed it, unless the Legislature, by adjournment, prevent such return.

Sec. 18. The Assembly shall have the sole power of impeachment; and all impeachments shall be tried by the Senate. When sitting for that purpose, the Senators shall be upon oath or affirmation; and no person shall be convicted, without the concurrence of two-thirds of the members present.

Sec. 19. The Governor, Lieutenant Governor, Secretary of State, Comptroller, Treasurer, Attorney General, Surveyor General, Justices of the Supreme Court and Judges of the District Courts, shall be liable to impeachment for any misdemeanor in office; but judgment in such cases shall extend only to removal from office, and disqualification to hold any office of honor, trust or profit, under the State; but the party convicted, or aquitted, shall nevertheless, be liable to indictment, trial, and punishment, according to law. All other civil officers shall be tried, for misdemeanors in office, in such manner as the Legislature may provide.

Sec. 20. No Senator, or member of Assembly, shall during the term for which he shall have been elected, be appointed to any civil office of profit, under this State, which shall have been created, or the emoluments of which shall have been increased, during such term, except such office as may be filled by elections by the people.

Sec. 21. No person holding any lucrative office under the United States, or any other power, shall be eligible to any civil office of profit, under this State: provided, that officers in the militia, to which there is attached no annual slarary, or local officers and postmasters whose compensation does not exceed five hundred dollars per annum, shall not be deemed lucrative.

Sec. 22. No person who shall be convicted of the embezzlement, or defalcation of the public funds of this State, shall ever be eligible to any office of honor, trust, or profit under this State; and the Legislature shall, as soon as practicable, pass a law providing for the punishment of such embezzlement, or defalcation, as a felony.

Sec. 23. No money shall be drawn from the treasury but in consequence of appropriations made by law. An accurate statement of the receipts and expenditures of the public moneys, shall be attached to and published with the laws at every regular session of the Legislature.

Sec. 24. The members of the Legislature shall receive for their services, a compensation to be fixed by law, and paid out of the public treasury; but no increase of the compensation shall take effect during the term for which the members of either house shall have been elected.

Sec. 25. Every law enacted by the Legislature shall embrace but one object, and that shall be expressed in the title; and no law shall be revised, or amended, by reference to its title; but in such case, the act revised, or section amended shall be re-enacted and published at length.

Sec. 26. No divorce shall be granted by the Legislature.

Sec. 27. No lottery shall be authorized by this State, nor shall the sale of lottery tickets be allowed.

Sec. 28. The enumeration of the inhabitants of this State shall be taken, under the direction of the Legislature, in the year one thousand eight hundred and fifty-two, and one thousand eight hundred and fifty-five, and at the end of every ten years thereafter; and these enumerations, together with the census that may be taken, under the direction of the Congress of the United States, in the year one thousand eight hundred and fifty, and every subsequent ten years, shall serve as the basis of representation in both houses of the Legislature.

Sec. 29. The number of Senators and members of Assembly, shall, at first session of the Legislature, holden after the enumerations herein provided for are made, be fixed by the Legislature, and apportioned among the several counties and districts to be established by law, according to the number of white inhabitants. The number of members of Assembly shall not be less than twenty four, nor more than thirty- six, until the number of inhabitants within this State, shall amount to one hundred thousand; and after that period, at such ratio that the whole number of members of Assembly shall never be less than thirty, nor more than eighty.

Sec. 30. When a congressional, senatorial, or assembly district, shall be composed of two or more counties, it shall not be separated by any county belonging to another district; and no county shall be divided, in forming a congressional, senatorial, or assembly district.

Sec. 31. Corporations may be formed under general laws, but shall not be created by special act, except for municipal purposes. All general laws and special acts passed pursuant to this section may be altered from time to time, or repealed.

Sec. 32. Dues from corporations shall be secured by such individual liability of the corporators, and other means, as may be prescribed by law.

Sec. 33. The term corporations as used in this article shall be construed to include all associations and joint-stock companies, having any of the powers or privileges of corporations not possessed by individuals or partnerships. And all corporations shall have the right to sue, and shall be subject to be sued, in all courts, in like cases as natural persons.

Sec. 34. The Legislature shall have no power to pass any act granting any charter for banking purposes; but associations may be formed, under general laws, for the deposite of gold and silver, but no such association shall make, issue, or put in circulation, any bill, check, ticket, certificate, promissory note, or other paper, or the paper of any bank, to circulate as money.

Sec.35. The Legislature of this State shall prohibit, by law, any person or persons, association, company, or corporation, from exercising the privileges of banking, or creating paper to circulate as money.

Sec. 36. Each stockholder of a corporation, or joint-stock association, shall be individually and personally liable for his proportion of all its debts and liabilities.

Sec. 37. It shall be the duty of the Legislature to provide for the organization of cities and incorporated villages, and to restrict their power of taxation, assessment, borrowing money, contracting debts, and loaning their credit, so as to prevent abuses in assessments and in contracting debts by such municipal corporations.

Sec. 38. In all elections by the Legislature, the members thereof shall voto viva voce, and the votes shall be entered on the journal.

ARTICLE V

Executive Department

Sec. 1. The supreme executive power of this State shall be vested in a Chief Magistrate, who shall be styled the Governor of the State of California.

Sec. 2. The Governor shall be elected by the qualified electors, at the time and places of voting for members of Assembly, and shall hold his office two years from the time of his installation, and until his successor shall be qualified.

Sec. 3. No person shall be eligible to the office of the Governor, (except at the first election) who has not been a citizen of the United States and a resident of this State two years next preceding the election, and attained the age of twenty-five years at the time of said election.

Sec. 4. The returns of every election for Governor shall be sealed up and transmitted to the seat of government, directed to the speaker of the Assembly, who shall, during the first week of the session, open and publish them in presence of both houses of the Legislature. The person having the highest number of votes shall be Governor; but in case any two or more have an equal and the highest number of votes, the Legislature shall, by joint vote of both houses, choose one of said persons, so having an equal and the highest number of votes, for Governor.

Sec. 5. The Governor shall be commander-in-chief of the militia, the army and navy of this State.

Sec. 6. He shall transact all executive business with the officers of Government, civil and military, and may require information in writing from the officers of the executive department, upon any subject relating to the duties of their respective offices.

Sec. 7. He shall see that the laws are faithfully executed.

Sec. 8. When any office shall, from any cause become vacant, and no mode is provided by the Constitution and laws for filling such vacancy, the Governor shall have power to fill such vacancy by granting a commission, which shall expire at the end of the next session of the Legislature, or at the next election by the people.

Sec. 9. He may, on extraordinary occasions, convene the Legislature by proclamation, and shall state to both houses, when assembled, the purpose for which they shall have been convened.

Sec. 10. He shall communicate by message to the Legislature, at every session, the condition of the State, and recommend such matters as he shall deem expedient.

Sec. 11. In case of a disagreement between the two houses, with respect to the time of adjournment, the Governor shall have power to adjourn the Legislature to such time as he may think proper; provided, it be not beyond the time fixed for the meeting of the next Legislature.

Sec. 12. No person shall, while holding any office under the United States, or this State, exercise the office of Governor, except as hereinafter expressly provided.

Sec. 13. The Governor shall have the power to grant reprieves and pardons after conviction, for all offences except treason and cases of impeachment, upon such conditions, and with such restrictions and limitations, as he may think proper, subject to such regulations as may be provided by law relative to the manner of applying for pardons. Upon conviction for treason he shall have the power to suspend the execution of the sentence until the case shall be reported to the Legislature at its next meeting, when the Legislature shall either pardon, direct the execution of the sentence, or grant a further reprieve. He shall communicate to the Legislature, at the beginning of every session, every case of reprieve or pardon granted, stating the name of the convict, the crime of which he was convicted , the sentence, and its date, and the date of the pardon or reprieve.

Sec. 14. There shall be a seal of this State, which shall be kept by the Governor, and used by him officially, and shall be called "The great seal of the State of California."

Sec. 15. All grants and commissions shall be in the name and by the authority of the people of the State of California, sealed with the great seal of the State, signed by the Governor and countersigned by the Secretary of State.

Sec. 16. A Lieutenant Governor shall be elected at the time and places, and in the same manner as the Governor; and his term of office, and his qualifications of eligibility shall also be the same. He shall be President of the Senate, but shall only have a casting vote therein. If, during a vacancy of the office of Governor, the Lieutenant Governor shall be impeached, displaced, resign, die or become incapable of performing the duties of his office, or be absent from the State, the President of the Senate shall act as Governor, until the vacancy be filled, or the disability shall cease.

Sec. 17. In case of the impeachment of the Governor, or his removal from office, death, inability to discharge the powers and duties of the said office, resignation, or absence from the State, the powers and duties of the office shall devolve upon the Lieutenant Governor for the residue of the term, or until the disability shall cease. But when the Governor shall, with the consent of the Legislature, be out of the State in time of war, at the head of any military force thereof, he shall continue commander-in-chief of the military force of the State.

Sec. 18. A Secretary of State, a Comptroller, a Treasurer, an Attorney General, and Surveyor General, shall be chosen in the manner provided in this Constitution; and the term of office, and eligibility of each shall be the same as are prescribed for the Governor and Lieutenant Governor.

Sec. 19. The Secretary of State shall be appointed by the Governor, by and with the advice and consent of the Senate. He shall keep a fair record of the official acts of the legislative and executive departments of the Government, and shall, when required, lay the same, and all matters relative thereto, before either branch of the Legislature; and shall perform such other duties as shall be assigned him by law.

Sec. 20. The Comptroller, Treasurer, Attorney General, and Surveyor General, shall be chosen by joint vote of the two houses of the Legislature, at their first session under this Constitution, and thereafter shall be elected at the same time and places, and in the same manner as the Governor and Lieutenant Governor.

Sec. 21. The Governor, Lieutenant Governor, Secretary of State, Comptroller, Treasurer, Attorney General, and Surveyor General, shall each at stated times during their continuance in office, receive for their services a compensation, which shall not be increased or diminished during the term for which they shall have been elected; but neither of these officers shall receive for his own use any fees for the performance of his official duties.

ARTICLE VI

Judicial Department

Sec. 1. The judicial power of this State shall be vested in a Supreme Court, in District Courts, in County Courts, and in Justices of the Peace. The Legislature may also establish such municipal and other inferior courts as may be deemed necessary.

Sec. 2. The Supreme Court shall consist of a Chief Justice and two Associate Justices, any two of whom shall constitute a quorum.

Sec. 3. The justices of the Supreme Court shall be elected at the general election, by the qualified electors of the State, and shall hold their office for the term of six years from the first day of January next after their election; provided that the Legislature shall, at its first meeting, elect a Chief Justice and two Associate Justices of the Supreme Court, by joint vote of both houses, and so classify them that one shall go out of office every two years. After the first election the senior Justice in commission shall be the Chief Justice.

Sec. 4. The Supreme Court shall have appellate jurisdiction in all cases when the matter in dispute exceeds two hundred dollars, when the legality of any tax, toll, or impost or municipal fine is in question, and in all criminal cases amounting to felony or questions of law alone. And the said Court, and each of the Justices thereof, as well as all district and county judges, shall have power to issue writs of habeas corpus at the instance of any person held in actual custody. They shall also have power to issue all other writs and process necessary to the exercise of their appellate jurisdiction, and shall be conservators of the peace throughout the State.

Sec. 5. The State shall be divided by the first Legislature into a convenient number of districts subject to such alteration from time to time as the public good may require, for each of which a district judge shall be appointed by the joint vote of the Legislature, at its first meeting, who shall hold his office for two years from the first day of January next after his election; after which, said judges shall be elected by the qualified electors of their respective districts, at the general election, and shall hold their office for the term of six years.

Sec. 6. The District Courts shall have original jurisdiction, in law and equity, in all civil cases where the amount in dispute exceeds two hundred dollars, exclusive of interest. In all criminal cases not otherwise provided for, and in all issues of fact joined in the probate courts, their jurisdiction shall be unlimited.

Sec. 7. The Legislature shall provide for the election, by the people, of a Clerk of the Supreme Court, and County Clerks, District Attorneys, Sheriffs, Coroners, and other necessary officers; and shall fix by law their duties and compensation. County Clerks shall be, ex officio, clerks of the District Courts in and for their respective counties.

Sec. 8. There shall be elected in each of the organized counties of this State, one County Judge, who shall hold his office for four years. He shall hold the County Court, and perform the duties of Surrogate, or Probate Judge. The County Judge, with two Justices of the Peace, to be designated according to law, shall hold courts of sessions, with such criminal jurisdiction as the Legislature shall prescribe, and he shall perform such other duties as shall be required by law.

Sec. 9. The County Courts shall have such jurisdiction, in cases arising in Justices Courts, and in special cases, as the Legislature may prescribe, but shall have no original civil jurisdiction, except in such special cases.

Sec. 10. The times and places of holding the terms of the Supreme Court, and the general and special terms of the District Courts within the several districts, shall be provided for by law.

Sec. 11. No judicial officer, except a Justice of the Peace, shall receive, to his own use, any fees or perquisites of office.

Sec. 12. The Legislature shall provide for the speedy publication of all statute laws, and of such judicial decisions as it may deem expedient; and all laws and judicial decisions shall be free for publication by any person.

Sec. 13. Tribunals for conciliation may be established, with such powers and duties as may be prescribed by law; but such tribunals shall have no power to render judgment to be obligatory on the parties, except they voluntarily submit their matters in difference, and agree to abide the judgment, or assent thereto in the presence of such tribunal, in such cases as shall be prescribed by law.

Sec. 14. The Legislature shall determine the number of Justices of the Peace, to be elected in each county, city, town, and incorporated village of the State, and fix by law their powers, duties, and responsibilities. It shall also determine in what cases appeals may be made from Justices Courts to the County Court.

Sec. 15. The Justices of the Supreme Court, and Judges of the District Court, shall severally, at stated times during their continuance in office, receive for their services a compensation, to be paid out of the treasury, which shall not be increased or diminished during the term for which they shall have been elected. The county Judges shall also severally, at stated times, receive for their services a compensation to be paid out of the county treasury of their respective counties, which shall not be increased or diminished during the term for which they shall have been elected.

Sec. 16. The Justices of the Supreme Court and District Judges shall be ineligible to any other office, during the term for which they shall have been elected.

Sec. 17. Judges shall not charge juries with respect to matters of fact, but may state the testimony and declare the law.

Sec. 18. The style of all process shall be "The People of the State of California;" all the prosecutions shall be conducted in the name and by the authority of the same.

ARTICLE VII

Militia

Sec. 1. The Legislature shall provide by law for organising and disciplining the militia, in such manner as they shall deem expedient, not incompatible with the Constitution and laws of the United States.

Sec. 2. Officers of the militia shall be elected, or appointed, in such a manner as the Legislature shall from time to time direct, and shall be commissioned by the governor.

Sec. 3. The governor shall have power to call forth the militia, to execute the laws of the State, to suppress insurrections, and repel invasions.

ARTICLE VIII

State Debts

The Legislature shall not in any manner create any debt or debts, liability or liabilities, which shall singly, or in the aggregate, with any previous debts or liabilities, exceed the sum of three hundred thousand dollars, except in case of war, to repel invasion or suppress insurrection, unless the same shall be authorised by some law for some single object or work, to be distinctly specified therein, which law shall provide ways and means, exclusive of loans, for the payment of the interest of such debt or liability, as it falls due, and also pay and discharge the principal of such debt or liability within twenty years from the time of the contracting thereof, and shall be irrepealable until the principal and interest thereon shall be paid and discharged; but no such law shall take effect until, at a general election, it shall have been submitted to the people, and have received a majority of all the votes cast for and against it at such election; and all money raised by authority of such law, shall be applied only to the specific object therein stated, or to the payment of the debt thereby created; and such law shall be published in at least one newspaper in each judicial district, if one be published therein, throughout the State, for three months next preceding the election at which it is submitted to the people.

ARTICLE IX

Education

Sec. 1. The Legislature shall provide for the election, by the people, of a superintendent of public instruction, who shall hold his office for three years, and whose duties shall be prescribed by law, and who shall receive such compensation as the Legislature may direct.

Sec. 2. The Legislature shall encourage, by all suitable means, the promotion of intellectual, scientific, moral and agricultural improvement. The proceeds of all land that may be granted by the United States to this State for the support of schools, which may be sold or disposed of, and the five hundred thousand acres of land granted to the new States, under an act of Congress distributing the proceeds of the public lands among the several States of the Union, approved A.D. 1841; and all estates of deceased persons who may have died without leaving a will, or heir, and also such per cent. as may be granted by Congress on the sale of lands in this State, shall be and remain a perpetual fund, the interest of which, together with all the rents of the unsold lands, and such other means as the Legislature may provide, shall be inviolably appropriated to the support of common schools throughout the State.

Sec. 3. The Legislature shall provide for a system of common schools, by which a school be kept up and supported in each district at least three months in every year, and any school neglecting to keep and support such a school, may be deprived of its proportion of the interest of the public fund during such neglect.

Sec. 4. The Legislature shall take measures for the protection, improvement, or disposition of such lands as have been, or may hereafter be reserved of granted by the United States, or any person of persons to the State for the use of a University; and the funds accruing from the rents or sale of such lands, or from any other source for the purpose aforesaid, shall be and remain a permanent fund, the interest of which shall be applied to the support of said University, with such branches as the public convenience may demand, for the promotion of literature, the arts and sciences, as may be authorised by the terms of such grant. And it shall be the duty of the Legislature, as soon as may be, to provide effectual means for the improvement and permanent security of the funds of said University.

ARTICLE X

Mode of Amending and Revising the Constitution

Sec. 1. Any amendment, or amendments to this Constitution, may be proposed in the Senate or Assembly; and if the same shall be agreed to by a majority of the members elected to each of the two houses, such proposed amendments, shall be entered on their journals, with the yeas and nays taken thereon, and referred to the Legislature then next to be chosen, and shall be published for three months next preceding the time of making such choice. And if, in the Legislature next chosen as aforesaid, such proposed amendment of amendments, shall be agreed to by a majority of all the members elected to each house, then it shall be the duty of the Legislature to submit such proposed amendment of amendments to the people, in such manner, and at such time as the Legislature shall prescribe; and if the people shall approve and ratify such amendment or amendments, by a majority of the electors qualified to vote for members of the Legislature, voting thereon, such amendment of amendments, shall become part of the Constitution.

Sec. 2. And if, at any time two-thirds of the Senate and Assembly shall think it necessary to revise and change this entire Constitution, they shall recommend to the electors, at the next election for members of the Legislature, to vote for or against the convention; and if it shall appear that a majority of the electors voting at such election have voted in favor of calling a convention, the Legislature shall, at its next session, provide by law for calling a convention, to be holden within six months after the passage of such law; and such convention shall consist of a number of members not less than that of both branches of the Legislature.

ARTICLE XI

Miscellaneous Provisions

Sec. 1. The first session of the Legislature shall be at the Pueblo de San Jose; which place shall be the permanent seat of government, until removed by law: Provided, however, that two-thirds of all members elected to each house of the Legislature shall concur in the passage of such law.

Sec. 2. Any citizen of this State who shall, after the adoption of this Constitution, fight a duel with deadly weapons, or send, or accept a challenge to fight a duel with deadly weapons, either within this State or out of it; or who shall act as second, or knowingly aid or assist in any manner those thus offending, shall not be allowed to hold any office of profit, or to enjoy the right of suffrage under this Constitution.

Sec. 3. Members of the Legislature, and all officers, executive and judicial, except such inferior officers as may be by law exempted, shall, before they enter on the duties of their respective officers, take and subscribe the following oath or affirmation:

" I do solemnly swear (or affirm, as the case may be,) that I will support the Constitution of the United States, and the Constitution of the State of California, and that I will faithfully discharge the duties of the office of , according to the best of my ability."

And no other oath, declaration, or test, shall be required as a qualification for any office or public trust.

Sec. 4. The Legislature shall establish a system of county and town governments, which shall be as nearly as practicable, throughout the State.

Sec. 5. The Legislature shall have the power to provide for the election of a board of supervisors in each county; and these supervisors shall jointly and individually perform such duties as may be prescribed by law.

Sec. 6. All officers whose election or appointment is not provided for by this Constitution, and all officers whose offices may hereafter be created by law, shall be elected by the people, or appointed as the Legislature may direct.

Sec. 7. When the duration of any office is not provided for by this Constitution, it may be declared by law, and if not so declared, such office shall be held during the pleasure of the authority making the appointment; nor shall the duration of any office not fixed by this Constitution ever exceed four years.

Sec. 8. The fiscal year shall commence on the 1st day of July.

Sec. 9. Each county, town, city, and incorporated village, shall make provision for the support of its own officers, subject to such restrictions and regulations as the Legislature may prescribe.

Sec. 10. The credit of the State shall not, in any manner, be given or loaned to or in aid of any individual, association, or corporation; nor shall the State directly of indirectly become a stockholder in any association or corporation.

Sec. 11. Suits may be brought against the State in such manner, and in such courts, as shall be directed by law.

Sec. 12. No contract of marriage, if otherwise duly made, shall be invalidated for want of conformity to the requirements of any religious sect.

Sec. 13. Taxation shall be equal and uniform throughout the State. All property in this State shall be taxed in proportion to its value, to be ascertained as directed by law; but assessors and collectors of town, county, and State taxes, shall be elected by the qualified electors of the district, county, or town, in which the property taxed for State, county, or town purposes is situated.

Sec. 14. All property, both real and personal, of the wife, owned or claimed by marriage, and that acquired afterwards by gift, devise, or descent, shall be her separate property; and laws shall be passed more clearly defining the rights of the wife, in relation as well to her separate property as to that held in common with her husband. Laws shall also be passed providing for the registration of the wife's separate property.

Sec. 15. The Legislature shall protect by law, from forced sale, a certain portion of the homestead and other property of all heads of families.

Sec. 16. No perpetuities shall be allowed, except for eleemosynary purposes.

Sec. 17. Every person shall be disqualified from holding any office of profit in this State, who shall have been convicted of having given, or offered a bribe, to procure his election or appointment.

Sec. 18. Laws shall be made to exclude from office, serving on juries, and from the right of suffrage, those who shall hereafter be convicted of bribery, perjury, forgery, or other high crimes. The privilege of free suffrage shall be supported by laws regulating elections, and prohibiting, under adequate penalties, all undue influence thereon from power, bribery, tumult, or other improper practice.

Sec. 19. Absence from this State on business of the State, or of the United States, shall not affect the question of residence of any person.

Sec. 20. A plurality of the votes given at an election shall constitute a choice, where not otherwise directed in this Constitution.

Sec. 21. All laws, decrees, regulations, and provisions, which from their nature require publication, shall be published in English and Spanish.

ARTICLE XII

Boundary

The Boundary of the State of California shall be as follows :

Commencing at this point of intersection of 42d degree of north latitude with the 120th degree of longitude west from Greenwich, and running south on the line of said 120th degree of west longitude until it intersects the 39th degree of north latitude; thence running in a straight line in a south easterly direction to the River Colorado, at a point where it intersects the 35th degree of north latitude; thence down the middle of the channel of said river, to the boundary line between the United States and Mexico, as established by the Treaty of May 30th, 1848; thence running west and along said boundary line to the Pacific Ocean, and extending therein three English miles; thence running in a northwesterly direction, and following the direction of the Pacific Coast to the 42d degree of north latitude, thence on the line of said 42d degree of north latitude to the place of beginning. Also all the islands, harbors, and bays, along adjacent to the Pacific Coast.

Schedule

Sec. 1. All rights, prosecutions, claims and contracts, as well of individuals as of bodies corporate, and all laws in force at the time of the adoption of this Constitution, and not inconsistent therewith, until altered or repealed by the Legislature, shall continue as if the same had not been adopted.

Sec. 2. The Legislature shall provide for the removal of all causes which may be pending when this Constitution goes into effect, to courts created by the same.

Sec. 3. In order that no inconvenience may result to the public service, from the taking effect of this Constitution, no office shall be superceded thereby, nor the laws relative to the duties of the several officers be changed, until the entering into office of the new officers to be appointed under this Constitution.

Sec. 4. The provisions of this Constitution concerning the term of residence necessary to enable persons to hold certain offices therein mentioned, shall not be held to apply to officers chosen by the people at the first election, or by the Legislature at its first session.

Sec. 5. Every citizen of California, declared a legal voter by this Constitution, and every citizen of the United States, a resident of this State on the day of election, shall be entitled to vote at the first general election under this Constitution, and on the question of the adoption thereof.

Sec. 6. This Constitution shall be submitted to the people, for their ratification or rejection, at the general election to be held on Tuesday, the thirteenth day of November next. The Executive of the existing Government of California is hereby requested to issue a proclamation to the people, directing the Prefects of the several districts, or in case of vacancy, the Sub-Prefects, or senior Judge of first Instance, to cause such election to be

*The 1849 State Constitution was California's first state constitution. The State currently operates under a constitution adopted in 1879.

held, the day aforesaid, in the respective districts. The election shall be conducted in the manner which was prescribed for the election of Delegates to this Convention, except that the Prefect, Sub-Prefect, or senior Judge of first Instance ordering such election in each district, shall have power to designate any additional number of places for opening the polls, and that, in every place of holding the election, a regular poll-list shall be kept by the judges and inspectors of election. It shall also be the duty of these judges and inspectors of election, on the day aforesaid, to receive the votes of the electors qualified to vote at such election. Each voter shall express his opinion, by depositing in the ballot-box a ticket, whereon shall be written, or printed "For the Constitution," or "Against the Constitution," or some such words as will distinctly convey the intention of the voter. These Judges and Inspectors shall also receive the votes for the several officers to be voted for at the said election as herein provided. At the close of the election, the judges and Inspectors shall carefully count each ballot, and forthwith make duplicate returns thereof to the Prefect, Sub-Prefect, or senior Judge of first Instance, as the case may be, of their respective districts; and said Prefect, Sub-Prefect, or senior Judge of first Instance shall transmit one of the same, by the most safe and rapid conveyance, to the Secretary of State. Upon the receipt of said returns, or on the tenth day of December next, if the returns be not sooner received, it shall be the duty of a board of canvassers, to consist of the Secretary of State, one of the Judges of the Superior Court, the Perfect, Judge of first Instance, and an Alcalde of the District of Monterey, or any three of the aforementioned officers, in the presence of all who shall choose to attend, to compare the votes given at said election, and to immediately publish an abstract of the same in one or more of the newspapers of California. And the Executive will also immediately after ascertaining that the Constitution has been ratified by the people, make proclamation of the fact; and thenceforth this Constitution shall be ordained and established as the Constitution of California.

Sec. 7. If this Constitution shall be ratified by the people of California, the Executive of the existing government is hereby requested immediately after, the same shall be ascertained, in the manner herein directed, to cause a fair copy thereof to be forwarded to the President of the United States, in order that he may lay it before the Congress of theUnited States.

Sec. 8. At the general election aforesaid, viz: the thirteenth day of November next, there shall be elected a Governor, Lieutenant-Governor, members of the Legislature, and also two Members of Congress.

Sec. 9. If this Constitution shall be ratified by the People of California, the Legislature shall assemble at the seat of government on the fifteenth day of December next, and in order to complete the organization of that body, the Senate shall elect a President pro tempore, until the Lieutenant-Governor shall be installed into office.

Sec. 10. On the organization of the Legislature, it shall be the duty of the Secretary of State, to lay before each house, a copy of the abstract made by the board of canvassers, and if called for, the original returns of election, in order that each house may judge of the correctness of the report of said board of canvassers.

Sec. 11. The Legislature, at its first session, shall elect such officers as may be ordered by this Constitution, to be elected by that body, and within four days after it organization, proceed to elect two Senators to the Congress of the United States. But no law passed by this Legislature shall take effect until signed by the Governor after his installation into office.

Sec. 12. The Senators and Representatives to the Congress of the United State, elected by the Legislature and People of California, as herein directed, shall be furnished with certified copies of this Constitution, when ratified, which they shall lay before the Congress of the United States, requesting, in the name of the People of California, the admission of the State of California into the American Union.

Sec. 13. All officers of this State, other than members of the Legislature, shall be installed into office on the fifteenth day of December next, or as soon thereafter as practicable.

Sec. 14. Until the Legislature shall divide the State into counties, and senatorial and assembly districts, as directed by this Constitution, the following shall be the apportionment of the two houses of the Legislature, viz: the districts of San Diego and Los Angelos, shall jointly elect two senators; the districts of Santa Barbara and San Luis Obispo, shall jointly elect one senator; the district of Monterey, one senator; the district of San Jose, one senator; the district of San Francisco, two senators, the district of Sonoma, one senator; the district of Sacramento, four senators; and the district of San Joaquin, four senators. And the district of San Diego shall elect one member of assembly; the district of Los Angelos, two members of assembly; the district of Santa Barbara, two members of assembly; the district of San Luis Obispo, one member of assembly; the district of Monterey, two members of assembly: the district of San Jose, three members of assembly; district of San Francisco, five members of assembly; the district of Sonoma, two members of assembly ; the district of Sacramento, nine members of assembly; and the district of San Joaquin nine members of assembly.

Sec. 15. Until the Legislature shall otherwise direct, in accordance with the provisions of this Constitution, the salary of the Governor shall be ten thousand dollars per annum; and the salary of the Lieutenant-Governor shall be double the pay of a State senator; and the pay of members of the Legislature shall be sixteen dollars per diem, while in attendance, and sixteen dollars for every twenty miles travel by the usual route from their residences, to the place of holding the session of the Legislature, and in returning therefrom. And the Legislature shall fix the salaries of all officers, other than those elected by the people, at the first election.

Sec. 16. The limitation of the powers of the Legislature, contained in article 8th of this Constitution, shall not extend to the first Legislature elected under the same, which is hereby authorised to negotiate for such amount as may be necessary to pay the expenses of the State Government.

R. SEMPLE, President of the Convention, and Delegate from Benicia.

Wm. G. Marcy, Secretary.

J. ARAM,

B. S. LIPPINCOTT

C. T. BOTTS,

M. M. McCARVER,

E. BROWN,

JOHN McDOUGAL,

J. A. CARRILLO,

B.F. MOORE,

J. M. COVARRUBIAS,

MYRON NORTON,
E. O. CROSBY,
P. ORD,
P. DE LA GUERRA,
MIGUEL PEDRORENA,
L. DENT,
A. M. PICO,
M. DOMINGUEZ,
R. M. PRICE,
K. H. DIMMICK,
HUGO REID,
A. J. ELLIS,
JACINTO RODRIGUEZ,
S. C. FOSTER,
PEDRO SANSEVAINE,
E. GILBERT,
W. E. SHANNON,
W. M. GWIN,
W. S. SHERWOOD,
H. W. HALLECK,
J. R. SNYDER,
JULIAN HANKS,
A. STEARNS,
L. W. HASTINGS,
W. M. STEUART,
HENRY HILL,
J. A. SUTTER,
J. HOBSON,
HENRY A. TEFFT,
J. McH. HOLLINSWORTH,
S. L. VERMULE,
J. D. HOPPE,
M. G. VALLEJO,
J. M. JONES,
J. WALKER,
T. O. LARKIN,
O. M. WOZENCRAFT,
FRANCIS J. LIPPITT.

California Counties
in the year 1850

1. Trinity
2. Shasta
3. Mendocino
4. Colusa
5. Butte
6. Sonoma
7. Napa
8. Yolo
9. Sutter
10. Yuba
11. Marin
12. Solano
13. Sacramento
14. El Dorado
15. San Francisco
16. Contra Costa
17. San Joaquin
18. Calaveras
19. Santa Cruz
20. Santa Clara
21. Tuolumne
22. Monterey
23. San Luis Obispo
24. Santa Barbara
25. Los Angeles
26. Mariposa
27. San Diego

California Counties
in the year 2000

1. Del Norte
2. Siskiyou
3. Modoc
4. Humboldt
5. Trinity
6. Shasta
7. Lassen
8. Mendocino
9. Tehama
10. Plumas
11. Lake
12. Glenn
13. Butte
14. Sierra
15. Colusa
16. Sutter
17. Yuba
18. Nevada
19. Sonoma
20. Napa
21. Yolo
22. Placer
23. El Dorado
24. Marin
25. Solano
26. Sacramento
27. Amador
28. Alpine
29. San Francisco
30. Contra Costa
31. San Joaquin
32. Calaveras
33. Tuolumne
34. San Mateo
35. Alameda
36. Stanislaus
37. Mariposa
38. Mono
39. Santa Cruz
40. Santa Clara
41. Merced
42. Madera
43. Monterey
44. San Benito
45. Fresno
46. Inyo
47. Kings
48. Tulare
49. San Luis Obispo
50. Kern
51. San Bernadino
52. Santa Barbara
53. Ventura
54. Los Angeles
55. Orange
56. Riverside
57. San Diego
58. Imperial

Recommended books for further reading

Batman, Richard. *The Outer Coast*, New York: Harcourt Brace Jovanovich, 1985.

Bauer, K. Jack. *Mexican War 1846-1848*, New York: MacMillan, 1974.

Bell, Horace. *Reminiscences of a Ranger*, Los Angeles: The Primavera Press, 1881.

Bristow, Gwen, *Calico Palace*, New York: Thomas Crowell Co., 1970

Bidwell, John. *Life in California Before the Gold Discovery*, Palo Alto: Lewis Osborne, 1966 (Ltd. Edition).

Buje, Emil T.H.. *Pre-Marshall Gold in California*, Sacramento: Historic California Press, 1983.

Cannon, Ray. *The Sea of Cortez*, Menlo Park, CA: Sunset Book, 1966.

Carrillo, Leo, *The California I Love*, Englewood Cliffs, NJ: Prentice-Hall, Inc., 1961.

Caughey, John. *California*, 3rd Ed., Englewood Cliffs, NJ: Prentice-Hall, Inc., 1970.

Chester, Michael. *Forts of Old California*, New York: G.P. Putnam & Sons, 1966.

Coblentz, Stanton. *Villains and Violantes*, New York: Thomas Yoseloff, Inc., 1936.

Copley, James. *The Call to California*, San Diego: The Union Tribune Publishing Co., 1968.

Davison, Michael (Ed.). *When, Where, Why, and How it Happened*, London: Reader's Digest General Books, 1993.

Engstrand, Iris H.W. *San Diego—California Cornerstone*, Tulsa, OK: Silvey and Drown, 1980.

Forquhar, P. *History of the Sierra Nevada*, Los Angeles: University of California Press, 1965.

Garst, Shannon. *Kit Carson*, New York: Julian Messner, Inc., 1942.

Gillett, Paul and Peter Odens. *Imperial Valley's Lost Gold*, Yuma, AZ: Southwest Printers, 1974.

Gleason, Duncan. *Islands and Ports of California*, New York: Devin-Adair Co., 1958.

Griswold del Castillo, Richard. *Treaty of Guadalupe Hidalgo*, Norman, OK: University of Oklahoma Press, 1990.

Halleck, Henry W. *The Mexican War in Baja California*, Larchmont, LA: Dawson's Book Shop, 1977.

Hunt, Thomas, H. *Ghost Trails to California*, Palo Alto, CA: American West, 1974.

Huntington, Harriet. *California Harbors*, Garden City, NY: Doubleday and Co., 1964

Jameson, W. C.. *Buried Treasure of California*, Little Rock, AR: August House Publisher, 1995.

Johnson, Paul. *Pictorial History of California*, New York: Doubleday, Inc., 1970.

Johnson, William Weber. *The Battle of San Pasqual*, San Diego: Pembroke Publishers, 1972.

Johnson, William Weber. *Baja California*, Alexandria, VA: Time-Life Books, 1972.

Kelly, Don Greame. *Edge of a Continent*, Palo Alto, CA: American West, 1971.

Klein, Javits. *Where to Find Gold in Southern California*, Baldwin, CA: Gem Guides Book Co., 1994.

Knight, Donald and Eugene Wheeler. *Agony and Death on a Gold Rush Steamer*, Ventura, CA: Pathfinder Publishing, 1990.

Lewis, Ernest Allen. *The Fremont Cannon*, Glendale: Arthur H. Clark, 1981.

Lewis, Oscar. *Sutter's Fort*, Englewood Cliffs, NJ: Prentice-Hall, Inc. 1966.

Lydon, Sandy. *Chinese Gold*, Capitola, CA: Capitola Book Co., 1985.

Maas, P. *When California Was an Island*, Santa Clara, CA: Storyline Press, 1953.

Marti, Werner. *Messenger of Destiny: The California Adventure of Archibald Gillespie.*

Nelson, Maidee. *California, Land of Promise*, Caldwell, ID: The Caxton Printers, Ltd., 1962.

Pepper, Choral and Brad Williams. *Lost Legends of the West*, New York: Holt, Rinehart, & Winston, 1970.

Polk, Dora Beale. *The Island of California*, Lincoln, NE: The University of Nebraska Press, 1991.

Pourade, Richard. F. *The Explorers: The History of San Diego*, San Diego: Union-Tribune, 1960.

Reinstedt, Randall. *Mysterious Sea Monsters of California's Central Coast*, Carver, CA: Ghost Town Publications, 1979.

Rosenus, Alan. *General Vallejo*, Berkeley: Heyday Books, 1995.

Robinson, W.W. *Land in California*, Berkeley, CA: University of California Pr. 1948.

Rolle, Andrew. *California History*, 4th Ed., Wheeling, IL: Harlan Davidson, Inc., 1987.

Roske, Ralph. *Everyman's Eden*, New York: MacMillan Co., 1968.

Sheafer, Silvia Ann. *Chinese and the Gold Rush*, Whittier, CA: Journal Publications, 1979.

White, Stewart Edward. *The Story of California*, Garden City, NY: Doubleday, Inc., 1948.

Wurlitzer, Rudy. *Walker*, New York: Harper & Row Publishers, 1987.

Zauner, Phyllis and Lou. *California Gold*, Tahoe Pacadwe, CA: Zanel Publications, 1980.

~ORDER FORM~

If you would like to order additional copies of this book, you may order them from the author or the publisher, simply by filling out this order form and sending it along with your check or money order.

Mr. Tom Elliott
546 Clarence Lane
Escondido, CA 92029

OR

Barbed Wire Publishing
1990 E. Lohman, Suite 225
Las Cruces, NM 88001
888.817.1990 (toll free)
e-mail: thefolks@barbed-wire.net
www.barbed-wire.net

- -

YES, I would like to order!

_____ copies of *Argonauts of California*, at $19.95 per copy, plus $3.50 shipping & handling for each book.

Send the book(s) to:

NAME ____

STREET ADDRESS ______________________________________

CITY ____________________________ STATE _____ ZIP __________

PHONE/E-MAIL _______________________________________